DIVINE MOMENTS

Fascinating Moments from the Other Side

Barbara Larter

GLASS HOUSE PUBLICATIONS ~ SAN DIEGO

Published by Glass House Publications
Text Copyright © 2012 by Barbara Larter
Photo Copyright © 2012 by Barbara Larter

www.glasshousepublications.com

ISBN 978-0-9890733-0-1

Manufactured in the United States of America

First Paperback Edition: April 2013

Acknowledgments

I thank God, without whose intervention in our lives this book could never have been written.

I thank Cherry Kovacovich for editing and seeing to it that this book was published.

I thank Cheryl Weisenberger for proofreading the manuscript.

I thank my wonderful husband, Jim, for giving up his office so I could keep all my papers together.

Contents

Introduction

Introduction

I never thought I would write a book. After talking to my pastor and a psychiatrist to find out if I was losing my mind, I decided I'd tell some of my close relatives and friends about my visions. They all rolled their eyes, said I was just dreaming or I just don't believe it. This was very disheartening to me because I knew these things were really happening to me.

When you have visions, they affect you so much that you just can't keep them from your mind. But to be quite honest, if I hadn't experienced them, I probably wouldn't have believed that they were real either.

Several years after my visions had stopped, and I was still talking about them, my supervisor at work, my relatives, and a few friends said, "You should write a book." Of course, I said, "I don't know how to write a book!" I explain how I changed my mind in one of my "Divine Moments."

Most of my visions have been so clear that I thought they were actual people or animals in my room. Some spirits were rather gray and farther away and faded quickly. Some were near the ceiling or at the top part of the walls and were harder for me to see. Most of them, however, were just above my eye level while I was lying in bed.

I understand from all of my readings that materializing enough for us to see them is challenging for the spirits from the other side. Since materializing seems to be challenging for them, and the newly "passed over" may have to try harder.

I hope you enjoy what I have experienced and written about. Maybe it will even inspire you to do the same or at least open your mind to these happenings, which are fascinating. If nothing else, this studying, reading, and writing of this book have certainly increased my faith in the afterlife and my belief in God.

There are only two ways to live:
One is as though nothing is a miracle,
The other is as if everything is.

…Albert Einstein

Part 1

Divine Moments

- Those little nudges from God that lovingly
direct your life.

Coincidences or Divine Moments?

July, 1953

I had just graduated from high school and had pretty
much decided on The Ohio State University for
my college career. My brother Doug was with the
Army in Europe. Dad and a friend, Frank O'Neil,
were going to see Doug in Germany and tour the
other countries. One day in late summer, Dad
asked me if I would like to accompany them to
Europe or to start college. After very little delibera-
tion, I said, "I'd really like to get started in college."

About the 21st of September 1953, Dad took me to
Columbus to find my room in the dormitory (Baker
Hall). My roommates were there and we all met.
Their names were Judy and Sally. They were both
from other parts of Ohio. Dad left and the three of
us roommates began to get to know each other. We
unpacked our belongings, chose beds, and then
went out to eat at Ptomaine Tommie's.

The next day, Sally said that she had come to Ohio
State with two of her male classmates, and they
were going to meet that evening and converse on
what each thought about the school, city, and their
dorms. Sally asked if we, Judy and I, would like to
come along. We both said, "Yes."

We walked over to the Student Union and in just a
few minutes three fellows showed up. Two were
the fellows who had come down with Sally. The
third was the most handsome man I had ever seen.

1

His name was Jim Larter. I fell in love immediately! That night, I wrote a letter to Doug and told him I had met the man I was going to marry.

Jim had spent the last two and a half years in Japan with the Air Force before being discharged in early August. He had signed up for an on-campus apartment but when he arrived the apartment was no longer available. They sent him over to the stadium dorms where he found his bunkmate Kenny. Kenny was one of the boys that were from Sally's high school.

One of the last things Mother said to me before Dad and I left for Columbus was, "Look out for the veterans. There are a lot of them at Ohio State". Almost the first thing Jim said to me was, "I'm a veteran," and I thought, "Oh, no! He's one of them,"

We were married two years later and celebrated our fifty-seventh (57th) wedding anniversary in 2012.

A Long-Lost Treasure

July, 1961.

Jim and I lived in Columbus, Ohio, after our wedding. In just a few months, we decided we'd move back to Springfield (my home town). He got a job immediately, and we moved into one of my grandfather's rentals. I was very satisfied there. We were close enough to all of my family that we had frequent visitors, and we could visit any of them whenever we wished.

We soon began our family and had two children, Cherry and Rusty.

After years six years of wedded bliss and our perfect family, Jim wanted to finish his degree. He had attended some night classes at Wittenberg College but he really needed to go fulltime and start working at a better job. So many days he would come home and say, "I've heard of a good engineering school in Louisiana," or so and so "went to the University of Cincinnati," etc. Every time he talked about us moving, I had many reasons why we shouldn't move.

Then one day I decided, the next time he comes home with a bright idea about moving, I'm going to say yes – no matter where he wants to move. Well, it was only a few days before he came home all excited and began to tell me about New Mexico State University.

One of his co-workers had attended there and he said they had co-op work with White Sands Missile Range and college housing for families that were individual houses. I said, "OK!" We put our house on the market and thought we weren't going to sell it in time to get into the fall semester. Since God had already "Nodded" several times during this whole time, we sold the house in July and signed the papers in August. We rented a U-Haul trailer and moved within a week.

One day I was standing on the side the house watching the guys load the U-Haul so we could begin our trip to Las Cruces, New Mexico. They were loading the trailer from the front door and down the steps. All at once, I noticed a shiny object in the grass beside me. I picked it up and lo and behold! It was the cross that White Mom, my grandmother, had given me in high school. I had lost it some years ago and, of course, we had cut the grass many times while we lived there. I believe someone (God) wanted me to find that necklace before we moved.

Our Path Continued with Divine Moments

August, 1961

I loved the whole area of Las Cruces, and Jim started school while working at White Sands. He was prepared to stay five years to complete his engineering degree, but he worked so hard that he finished in three years.

About a year into Jim's schooling he was exhausted from going to classes in the daytime, working nights at White Sands and spending all his extra time studying. I told him that I would find a job and he could then concentrate on school.

Since the housing area was full of young mothers with babies, it was easy for me to find a baby sitter for my two primary school youngsters. I saw an ad for a job at the university bulletin board, and I had a job at New Mexico State University Library within a week. I was hired for acquisitions. I liked this work setting and my co-workers. I stayed two years and quit about a day before Jim graduated with honors.

Jim began interviewing all over the country. When the Dow Chemical Co. called him; they said they would like him to come to the Freeport, Texas, plant. Jim told them he would rather work at the Michigan plant. The Dow official told Jim that he would like him to come to the Texas plant, and if he didn't like it, they would fly him to Michigan.

I was eagerly waiting for his phone call after he left for Freeport, Texas. It finally came, and he said, "You are going to love this area!" So I said, "OK!" A few weeks later, we arrived in Lake Jackson, Texas. (Dow Chemical literally built the town of Lake Jackson.) It was a gorgeous, heavily treed town with winding streets and lots of new houses.

Jim loved his job. We met so many nice people and found a Lutheran church (a rarity in the South) in which we became very involved.

After two years, I wanted to go back to work. There was an ad in the Classifieds for a Library Tech at Brazosport Community College (now Brazosport University). I interviewed with Frances Pye, the head librarian. She taught me to catalog the books. (I was a cataloger for twenty-three years at three Universities.) At one point, Frances and I even investigated opening a business together. We didn't do that, but we did start the most successful stock investment company that was run entirely by women with no advisor in America.

I quit working at Brazosport College to be a stay-at-home mom for a while and Frances had an opportunity to go to another college in Alvin, Texas. She called me one evening and asked if I would like to be a cataloger at Alvin Jr. College.

This was going to be a large raise over the last place I worked. I conversed with Jim over this. He really didn't want me driving the thirty miles, but he final ly agreed. I worked there until I single-handedly-changed the whole library over from the Dewey Decimal system to the Library of Congress system.

We stayed in Lake Jackson until Jim's dad became seriously ill, and Jim thought we should ask for a transfer to Hanging Rock, Ohio. Jim's parents lived on a farm and he thought he could help them with the cattle, hay, and the garden. Jim's dad died very soon after we moved to Ohio. We've lived in Southern Ohio ever since.

The Accident That Didn't Happen

Summer, 1962

Jim and I were on our way home from a vacation trip out West. I don't remember the speed limit at that time, but it was probably seventy mph.

We were on a two-lane highway. There was a car approaching us from the opposite direction and one in front of us. We were following at a safe distance for the speed.

The car in front of us signaled a right turn. Instead of turning in the expected smooth move, he stopped dead on the highway (there was a car exiting from the side road where the car in front of us wanted to turn into that we didn't see). Jim slammed on the brakes and there were no brakes. We were both sure we were going to hit the back of the car in our lane or head-on with the one approaching. Jim instantly chose the rear-end collision.

The next thing we knew, we were on the other side of the scene. Jim looked into the rear-view mirror and said the same scenario was there, all except our car! He tried the brakes and they were one hundred percent okay. We were so shook-up that we had to stop the car and get hold of ourselves. We both know that our guardian angel was instrumental in saving us from death that day.

A Godly Happening

Early 1960's

While we were living in Lake Jackson, Texas, Cherry, our daughter, and Laura, a neighbor, were friends. This day I was sitting out front waiting for Jim to come home from work as I did every evening. Laura came riding by on Cherry's bike, and just as soon as she passed me, she hit the curb. She flew over the handlebar and hit the cement pretty hard.

Someone, maybe me, called the emergency squad. When the emergency squad came, they took her to the hospital. She was still unconscious.

All night long, I prayed that she would be all right. When I'd go to sleep, I'd wake up about every half hour and offer another prayer. Finally, about 3:00 a.m., I went to sleep and slept until morning.

I decided to go down to Laura's house and ask her parents how she was doing. Her dad said she had come out of the coma about 3 a.m. Coincidence? I don't think so.

Woody Hayes!

July, 1964

Jim, the kids and I were visiting Mother and Dad in Springfield, Ohio. Dad suggested we go for ice cream cones.

While we were waiting for a table at the restaurant Dad nudged me and said, "There's Woody Hayes." (Woody Hayes was a very famous Coach of The Ohio State University football team.) I said, "It is?" Dad said, "Go ask him for his autograph." I was so shy that I really didn't want to, but Dad said, "Go ahead."

So I went up to him at the counter and said, "Mr. Hayes, may I have your autograph?" He said, "Sure, what do you want me to write it on?" I gave him the only thing that was handy – a napkin.

It made my day. I'm such a sports fan. I never dreamed I'd see him off the football field.

Advance Notice

Early 1970's

We were still living in Lake Jackson, Texas, and rearing our children as best we could to be good Christians. We went to Sunday school and church almost every Sunday.

This Sunday morning, Jim and I were in our class, and I asked if they had heard that a very popular Senator from the Houston area had died the night before. Someone asked me how I knew that. They said they had read the paper and they hadn't seen it. I said that I didn't know how I knew it. Even I was amazed at what I had said.

The Senator died about three days later.

Divine Moments meet Employment

February, 1980

After we got settled in our beautiful house in Wheelersburg, Ohio, I joined several clubs, was playing softball, tennis, volleyball, and bowling in a league. I was very happy with my carefree style of life.

One evening, Jim was reading the paper and said, "Shawnee State University is looking for a library employee. Why don't you see if you can get it?" I said I didn't want to work. He said, "Just go see if they'll hire you."

So the next day I had an interview with the head librarian. He said he'd like to check my references. I gave him Frances Pye's name and phone number. He called me the next day and said, "You're hired. After that sterling recommendation, how could I not hire you?" When Jim came home, I said, "I got the damn job!"

I stayed at Shawnee State University for fifteen and a half years. You just can't ignore Divine Moments.

Saint Joseph

Spring, 1998

In October of 1991, we bought a beautiful estate,
which included a thirty-room mansion plus about
ten acres of lawn on the bank of the Ohio River. We
turned it into a Bed and Breakfast with a fine dining
restaurant. It was called the 100 Mile House.

After about seven years we longed for some peace
and quiet and put the property up for sale. We had
a lot of curious people, but none that had any real
interest or the money to buy it. It was on the market about one and a half years. We finally decided
to move into Wheelersburg and try to find a house
there. Jim kept going out to the 100 Mile House to
check everything out and be sure no one was breaking in or anything.

My Catholic friends at Shawnee State University
kept asking me if we had sold the property yet. I
had to keep telling them, "No we haven't." One of
them said, "I can tell you how to sell your house."

Of course, I was very interested in that, so I said,
"Tell me more!" She said, "You go to the monastery and ask them for a statue of Saint Joseph. You
will sell the property very quickly."

Being Lutheran, I doubted the whole thing, but at
this point I was ready to try anything. The next day
I went to the monastery, and when I told the nun
what I wanted, she said, "Oh, you're trying to sell a

13

house." I laughed and said, "Yes." Well, the plastic Saint Joseph statue cost $2.98.

That evening, about 7:00 p.m., Jim said he was going to go check on the property. I said I'd like to go with him. When we arrived, he entered the house, and I went to the Ohio River side of the house and "planted Saint Joseph" upside down (as I had been instructed) in my flowerbed. I said, "There you are Saint Joseph, do your stuff!"

About 10:00 a.m. the next morning, Jim was out cutting grass when our phone rang. The man told me his name and said he had just found out that the 100 Mile house was for sale. I nearly dropped my theeth when he said he wanted to buy it. I ran out to the yard Jim was cutting and handed him the phone. The deal was finished within a month. I just couldn't believe it! Thank you Saint Joseph.

Boone

May, 2006

I had been so lonely since I stopped working that I
really felt as if I needed to change my life. I finally
came up with the idea that I'd get a dog. I wanted
an older dog because I knew I wouldn't be able to
keep up with a puppy. The idea of housebreaking
and teaching all the commands were things that I
just didn't feel like doing again.

One afternoon, Vicki, our daughter-in-law came
by and said, "How would you like a dog?" I said,
"What kind?" She told me it was an older Golden
Retriever. I said, "Yes!" immediately.

Jim who was sitting next to me said, "No!" He
thought we were gone too much to take care of
a dog properly. I said that I really wanted it and
maybe we could just go see it. I also said he could
buy himself something that he wanted. He said,
"Okay".

I asked Vicki where it was and when we could go
see it. She called the people who had it right then.
They said, "Anytime." I said, "How about right
now?"

So after Vicki left, we went to the people's house.
We took the truck just in case we liked him. When
we went there and first saw him, he was tied to the
dining room table with a three-foot leash. She said

he had been tied outside for a long time. I thought this must have been devastating for him because that breed of dog craves company.

After she let him loose, he ran over and nudged Jim and then came over to me and laid his head in my lap. He was my dog! We asked when we could take him, and they said "Now." They gave us his leash, food, and several other small things. We put him in the truck and he sat in the back seat with his head between us all the way home.

We didn't even know if he was housebroken, but he was going to be an indoor dog. As it turned out, he was perfectly trained in everything but walking slowly on a leash. Training him to that took a while since at my age I really couldn't walk very fast. But we finally accomplished even that.

He made up to our cats immediately and our indoor cat trained him within a few days to tell us when she wanted food or to be let out.

We had an in-ground swimming pool and he was afraid of it. I swam everyday and coaxed him to come in, but he didn't want to. Jim came out one afternoon and put Boone's front feet on the top step. The next day, I tied a twenty-foot rope to his collar and began teaching him to swim. It took about three days before he leveled his body and was swimming correctly. He had been trying to stand on his back legs and swim. You should have seen the expression on his face when he realized that he had learned to swim correctly. I wish I had a picture of his smile.

From then on, he didn't want me to go into the deep end, and he would swim out to get me.

It turned out that he was wonderful with everyone who came into the house, and he made it clear to everyone that he was my protector. He loved the very young grandchildren and let them pet him anywhere. He turned out to be an ideal, very well trained dog. He was about six years old.

Four years later he died with his new Christmas toy under his paw on New Year's Eve. We buried him where the swimming pool had been filled in. I planted a weeping willow tree there, and we plan to plant daffodil bulbs on his grave.

A Chance to Witness

May, 2006

I was still looking for a job and had put in many applications. It seemed as if no one was going to hire me. I kept reading the Help Wanted ads in the paper and nothing seemed to fit me. There was this one ad that had been running for about thirty days. I wondered what a "driver" did and assumed that it was driving a bus and I didn't want to drive a bus.

Then one day I was desperate and I called the company and asked, "Exactly what does a driver do?" She told me that drivers drove either a company car or their own car and took people to doctor's appointments and hospitals. Then she said, "Is this something you'd be interested in?" I said, "Yes. Would it be all right if I bring down my resume now?" She said it would be fine, and I could fill out the application at the same time.

When I got to their office, several people met me with big smiles on their faces. Everyone seemed so happy to see me. I filled out the paper, interviewed with the supervisor and the owner of the business, and I was hired on the spot.

When I came into work the next day, something was said about my age. I told them I was seventy-two years old, and they all denied that I could be that old. I was very glad they thought that because I'm sure my age was keeping me from getting any other job.

18

This job turned out to be a wonderful opportunity for me to discuss religion with many people. It seems that most people want to talk about religion but are afraid of offending someone. I was told not to ask about the client's health or talk about politics or religion unless the client brought it up. Not a day passed without the clients saying something about religion so I could talk about it with them.

One lady I picked up was so very angry she was even screaming to the top of her lungs about her !@# ex-husband. I later found out they had been divorced for twenty-four years. I had the opportunity on that day to tell her that anger hurt her body and soul. She said, "What's a soul?" I told her, and the next time I picked her up, she was much calmer. The first thing she said to me was, "Tell me more about that soul." Another Divine Moment directed two lives.

Message from an Angel

July, 2011

While I was in Cornville, Arizona, visiting our daughter and her husband, I went to my favorite Angelic Channel, Barbara Evans. One of the things she told me was one of my angels was named Monica and I should be asking her for things I needed or wanted. Monica was waiting for me to ask. Barbara told me that Monica would be leaving white feathers for me to find.

One evening, after praying to God, I decided to talk to Monica. I asked her to show me a white feather so that I would absolutely know she was real and with me.

The next hot summer afternoon, I was sitting under my awning on the deck reading a book, as usual. I was getting too warm, so I started to get up. I turned to get my bottle of water and there lay a perfectly white, small round feather next to the water bottle. I said, "Thank you, Monica." I was completely astounded!

I Need More Proof

August, 2011

I had been looking for white feathers from my angel, Monica, each time I was outdoors. I saw lots of gray ones but no white ones. One evening after my prayers to God, I was telling Monica that I would like to see another white feather from her – just for verification.

The next afternoon as I was preparing to read out on the deck, I saw what I thought was a white feather falling through a ray of sunlight in the back yard. I began to chase it, and after several tries, I finally had it in my hand. It was very light gray. In the sunlight, it had looked white. I wondered if Monica had sent it, but I decided she hadn't since she said she'd be sending a white feather.

I read a while and then went in to fold some clothes. When I came out again, I sat down in my chair under my huge awning and began to remove my shoes. There between my shoes was a white feather. I knew for certain that this one was from Monica. "Thank you, Monica."

Angel Help, Just in Time

Sept. 2011

I started a new job as a cashier at a very busy chain store. I was having trouble remembering all the numbers that I needed to access my account and open my register. I was also having trouble concentrating on giving the correct change.

In my exasperation I thought, "Monica", my angel, "is waiting to help me". So I asked her to help me concentrate while I was at work. Surprise! Every time I called her in to help, my drawer balanced. What a wonderful gift she has been!

In the Right Place

April 2002

Our church door was recently painted an ugly gray. It had been a pretty varnished wood before.

My son mentioned that his last church (he is a minister) had crosses painted on the doors and they were beautiful. I asked him to get the key so that I could take a picture of them.

Paul, one of his friends, had the key and met us at the church. I was taking pictures while the two of them stood there talking. My ears perked up when I heard Paul say that the churches try to help each other by giving anything they have to whomever needs it.

Our Council President had just announced in church the day before that our interim pastor would stay in the area for two days a week if we could get some furniture for the parsonage.

I asked Paul if he had any furniture and he said he had a table and chairs sitting in his garage. I called a person from our church and told him about the furniture. He said Paul had already called him.

They picked up the table and chairs that evening. This is an example of a great Divine Moment. "Thank you, Lord."

Part 2

Spirit Visits

or Visions

2000 – My granddaughter gave birth to a healthy, beautiful, blond baby girl.
2001 – The surgeon got all the cancer, no chemo, and I was in remission.
2002 – My heart problem was being taken care of by a pill.
2003 – Money wasn't a problem since Jim, my husband, and I were both working.

All was well at our house.

OK! Then why did I start having visions? If anyone can answer this question, you'd make me the happiest person in the world. Then I would ask God to please let me have more visions.

Spring, 2003 My first sighting of a "ghost" or "spirit."

We were now living in Wheelersburg, Ohio. I was just going to bed, and Jim was still in the bathroom. The bedside table lamp was on. I was lying in bed when all of a sudden a black cat appeared over the foot of the bed. I was seeing the side view of the head and a very strong neck. His mouth was open and his huge teeth were showing. I thought to myself, "I should be very afraid," but I was too interested in observing him. I wanted Jim to come into the bedroom just to see if he could see this, but he didn't. I watched him for several seconds and all of a sudden he turned and looked straight at me (maybe one or two seconds) and then vanished. I then realized that it was not just a cat. It was a panther.

27

Spring, 2003 Sabrina for sure?

The first light of a new day was just starting to
brighten the bedroom when I awoke and saw Sabrina, our black
cat, by the side of the bed. I rose up and then saw
that she had something in her mouth. I got out of
bed and ran around the bed after her and yelled,
"Jim, turn on the light. Sabrina is in the bedroom
and she has something in her mouth, maybe a lizard
or snake." He turned on the light and *poof* she
was gone. Jim said he had put the cat out when we
came to bed. I went to look in the garage where
Sabrina slept, and she was still in her bed.

Spring, 2003 Nurse

I was asleep and I awoke suddenly. There standing by Jim's side of the bed was a tall woman in
an old-fashioned nurse's uniform. She had on a
nurse's cap and a brown sweater that looked hand
knit. She was holding a clipboard and a pen or pen-
cil. Her right hand was poised over the clipboard as
if she were writing something about Jim. She was
a big-boned woman with a large nose. I was afraid
at first, but I decided that I shouldn't be and just
lay there and watched her. I lay very still because I
thought if I moved, she would go away. She didn't
move. This lasted several minutes; then she vanished.

Spring, 2003 Boy, the night after the nurse sighting.

I awoke in the middle of the night and was looking right at a boy about twelve years old standing close to my side of the bed. He was crying and sobbing and rubbing his eyes with his fists. It seemed as if he were crying his heart out. He wasn't looking at anything, and he was turned almost sideways to the bed. He had on a flat cap (like a golfer's hat) and a brown sweater. Both the hat and the sweater looked as if they were made of wool. I had the impression that he also had on knickers. I watched for a few seconds, and then he vanished.

These last two visions rather frightened me because I thought something was going to happen to Jim.

Summer 2003 Psychic Interpretations

Cherry, my daughter, had been invited to a party where they were going to have a psychic and a medium, David and Patricia. Cherry, in turn, asked me to go. This was to be at Cherry's friends' house in Columbus, Ohio.

When it was my turn I went up the stairs to talk to them and, as I reached the top of the stairs, Patricia said, "Your dog said that you were a good mother." I immediately started to cry because we had had to put our beloved eighteen-and-a-half year old Samoyed, Frosty, to sleep years before and I had felt guilty ever since.

They also said that Jim had been injured in the First World War and died. The nurse probably represented Jim having been injured and in the hospital. They thought the boy was Jim's son.

They said they didn't know the significance of the cat sightings I'd had (see earlier visions). I thought the panther was on an insignia used in the military. I still haven't documented this for sure, but there were several insignias with black panthers from the First World War. I researched on line and everywhere else I could think of to find an insignia with this panther on it. I was able to find several, but none of them was the exact panther that I had seen.

Summer, 2003 A Prayer answered.

I was having one of my "worry all day" times. I was crying, alone, and I said out loud, "I need something soft and furry to hug."

I went to the back door and looked out into the yard and there, at the edge of our house, was a very large, black
Labrador retriever. He was sitting there waiting for me to invite him to come closer. I went outside and said, "Come on." He came running and acted as if I were his long lost friend. I named him Buddy. He stayed with me all day long.

When Jim came home we decided to go out for awhile. I put Buddy inside the fence. When we returned, he was gone. If this isn't God at work, I don't know what is! I haven't seen the dog since.

December, 2003 Another Cat

As I awoke I was looking right into the eyes of a mottled black cat. Her eyes were open very wide; in fact, they were a little scary. With how many cats, I'm wondering, are we sharing our bed?

June, 2004 Old Man.

It was the middle of the night and I awoke abruptly. There stood an old man with no shirt on. His chest and stomach were just a mass of wrinkles, as though he had lost a lot of weight. He had a small white mustache and a round face. He was smiling at me and with his right hand, palm up, he started toward my head. I thought he was going to lift my head. I jumped (I don't know if he touched me and that caused me to jump or not). Then he was gone. He looked like a friendly sort of fellow.

August 31, 2004 Wallpaper Magic.

As I woke up, I looked at the wallpaper in the bedroom. Instead of seeing the far-apart ivy pattern, I saw a fern pattern that was almost solid. I blinked my eyes a couple of times and the ivy came back. This vision was in black and white.

September 1, 2004 Mystery Chair.

As I awoke, I was looking at the wall in my bedroom. There was a plastic outdoor chair with a large double flower suspended in the seat back. I had never seen a chair with this pattern before. It was just sitting there. I blinked my eyes several times and it went away. This was in black and white.

By this time, I was sure I was crazy. I had never heard of people seeing things when they were awake. All I ever heard about was what they saw in their dreams.

I decided to talk to someone who might give me some insight into these happenings. My first thought was to call the pastor of our church. She came over that afternoon. I told her what was happening, and she asked me why I thought they were happening. I told her I was pretty sure that God was sending me messages that I just couldn't understand. I told her I thought I would understand all of them at some time, maybe not until I'm in Heaven. She asked how I would feel if these things stopped happening. I told her that I would feel that I had done something I shouldn't have and that God took them away from me.

I had been thinking these were hallucinations, but she told me that they were visions. She said hallucinations were very frightening and visions were not. She told me that visions happen to a lot of people – we just don't know their purpose.

I felt very much better after talking to our pastor and started looking forward to more visions.

September 3, 2004 Sabrina, surprise!

I was still in bed one morning, and had just answered the phone. As I hung up, Sabrina, the cat,
rattled a cord behind the bed. This is one of her
annoying ways to wake me. I didn't say anything
to her. She chortled to me by the foot of the bed. I
chortled back to her to let her know I was awake.

After I had dressed for the day, I was going to the
garage to put some packages in the car. As I opened
the garage door, Sabrina ran into the house. Jim had
never let her into the house the night before.

September 5, 2004 Mystery Chair, again.

I awoke about 2:00 a.m. and I was looking at the
same chair as I had seen on September 1st. It was
in an upright position beside a low window. There
were no dividers in the window so that it could be
raised or cross-hatching as if it had panes. The
chair came more than halfway up the window. The
wall of the house or building was white stucco.
There were a few scattered ferns up the wall. Then
the image went away. I didn't recognize the chair,
the window, or the building. There are very few
stucco houses or buildings in this part of Ohio.

I awoke what seemed like several hours later, but
it had not started to get light. There was the same
scene as before, but now there was another chair
right beside the first one. It was blurry but had the
same suspended flower pattern in the back of the
chair.

33

September 7, 2004 Another Strange Man in My Bedroom.

When I awoke I saw a man lying down. I wondered if he might be dead. He had a lined face that led me to think that he was probably in his fifties. He was not a slender man but not fat either. The scene faded and then he was standing up and laughing. Something else was becoming visible in the upper left quadrant of the picture, but I couldn't see it plainly. I opened my eyes to see a white casket. This was a little dim and it left quickly.

September 9, 2004 New Wallpaper?

I was lying in bed trying to get serious about getting up. I opened my eyes and was looking in to the far upper left of my bedroom and then I realized that our wallpaper didn't have red in it. What I was looking at was a bunch of red poinsettias.

September 10, 2004 New Picture.

As I awoke, I saw a strange picture hanging on the wall. Really it was two pictures connected to each other, top to bottom. The bottom one was an or- ange car. I couldn't see the other plainly enough to tell what it was, but I got the impression that it had some orange in it too.

I remembered a picture Rusty, my son, had in his room as a child and it seemed to be similar to the bottom picture.

The pictures were at the top of the wall next to the ceiling and were on a slant.

September 11, 2004 Frosty.

This was about dawn when the head and face of our late Samoyed, Frosty, appeared in the upper, center of the wall. (She died in about 1985).   She just appeared, but she did not move.

September 12, 2004 Cat.

Jim had just turned on the lights for us to get up. I said to myself, "I guess I'll see if anything shows up this morning." I opened my eyes and there was a small black cat bounding back and forth across the bed. It stayed visible longer than Frosty.

September 13, 2004 From the spirit world?

Upon awakening, I thought I'd open my eyes just in case someone was sending me a message from the spirit world. There were two pink pigs. These looked as if they were made of wood and connected by a string – as if you were going to hang them on a Christmas tree or something. They were very pleasant looking and I had the feeling that they were about six inches long. It was hard for me to see the one on the right, so I was supposing that it looked like the other one. These were in the upper center of my vision.

September 14, 2004 A Brown Throw.

In the morning, I opened my eyes and there was a
five by seven foot throw covering the wall. In the
middle was about a ten-foot eagle coming in for a
landing. (The ten feet would have been his real life
measurement). This scene stayed on quite a while.
I'd say at least a minute.

September 16, 2004 Another Throw.

This morning I saw the same throw, except the
eagle had been replaced by what looked like a Zulu
mask. This was quite large – possibly eighteen
inches high. This scene stayed on about five minutes.
While this was still before me, or maybe it was after
this went off, I heard the cat chortle again. I think
she wanted me to get up. Sabrina was still in the
garage.

September 19, 2004 Yet another throw.

This time the throw was decorated throughout with
men in helmets like the knights wore while jousting.
These helmeted men were evenly spaced all over
the throw. There was another color coming through.
I think it was orange. I've forgotten that detail.

**September 21, 2004 Foxes, Tiger Cat and a Pink
Chair**

There were two red foxes peeking around the corner
of something. To the right and below was a mon-

key. I could see the bottom of the throw, so I thought that maybe this would be the end of it.

This looked like a picture of a tiger-striped cat that had been bonded to a heavy cardboard and cut out in the shape of the cat. I have see examples of this type work here in Southern Ohio. I have never had one done.

There was a pink chair that had flowers all over it as part of the fabric. This was a small bedroom chair and was sitting right by my side of the bed. I was sorry that Jim was in the shower at this time because I wanted to see if he could see the chair. At least that brown throw was gone!

September 23, 2004

The cat meowed again about 7:00 a.m. Sabrina again was in the garage.

September 24, 2004

12:30 a.m.: I awoke looking at an old-fashioned washbasin and pitcher and sticking up out of the pitcher was a plastic spork (a spoon with tines like a fork). The spork's handle looked like a wooden spoon. The pitcher had a painting on the side. I think this was like a cameo instead of a flower and I had the impression that it was green.

3:30 a.m.: I awoke looking at a weather vane and a painted birdhouse underneath it.

5:30 a.m.: I again awoke looking at something. I had to concentrate to bring this one in clearly. It finally came into focus and it was a "helicopter" over a small bird that was flapping his wings frantically trying to fly against the wind from the helicopter. This vision lasted only a few seconds.

September 27, 2004

Midnight: There were two skeletons in the picture. One was a life-sized, not doing anything. The other one appeared to be about fifteen inches high and was running very fast. Then there was a trunk with the lid up and the small skeleton was sitting on the edge of it and slid down into it, bottom first. I thought it was interesting that this happened at the "stroke of midnight" (as the scary movies always say.) The vision was not scary to me.

5:30 a.m.: I think I woke up because it was time for Jim to get up. Maybe he moved and that's why I awoke. Anyway, again the wallpaper turned into fern wallpaper. But this time the fern fronds were much larger and may have covered only the top half of the room.

September 29, 2004

Tonight's vision was a line drawing of a face. I got the impression that it was a woman. It was done in white on black. Then the brown throw showed up! The background was fern and I don't know what animal was in the middle.

September 30, 2004

The brown throw appeared again – just the middle part. This was a lady. I could see everything but her feet. She was clothed in linen dishtowels, white with blue stripes. Even her head was wrapped, but not her face. She looked at me and knew I was awake; then she looked at Jim and vanished.

October 4, 2004

I awoke at 12:45 a.m. I had been sleeping on my stomach and when I do that, I prop my pillow up against the headboard. After I put my pillow down on the bed and looked to see what time it was, that's when I saw the "present." It was a box, about twelve by twelve by three, wrapped in red paper with a red, white, and pink ribbon. I thought to myself, "I wonder if I can touch that since it was so close." I tried to touch it and my hand went right through it then it disappeared.

October 20, 2004

I haven't had any visions since we left for our vacation in Arizona. I think I have been just too tired to be receptive. So I was surprised when this one came through soon after we arrived home.

Tonight's vision started in the corner of our bedroom. It was two shiny bowl-type items, one on top of the other. The only thing I could think that this was an old-fashioned percolator coffee pot, probably made of chrome by Sunbeam. Every coffee lover had one of these in the fifties and sixties. Then I looked around and there was the fern "wall-paper." I felt happy when I saw this because I was afraid the spirits had left me. (This happened after Jim woke me in the morning. When he turned on the light, the images left.)

October 21, 2004

I awakened about 3:00 a.m. I had been sleeping on my stomach and it was time to turn over. As I raised my head off the bed to put the pillow down on the bed, I noticed the sheets and pillowslip had print design – tiny yellow flowers with green leaves. I smiled because my sheets are solid blue. As I turned over, I saw the fern "wallpaper."

October 22, 2004

I don't have any sense of what time it was when I awoke, but there was a large (four inches by ten inches) beetle-type hard-shell bug that was walking up under a white window shade. The vision ended when he disappeared behind the shade.

October 25, 2004

All I saw tonight was just a quick glimpse of the fern wallpaper, but this time my bedspread also had ferns for the pattern.

October 29, 2004

Tonight's vision was another with the brown throw.

This time there was a man's face. It could have been Jesus but not exactly like the pictures we see. The other was a moose, large antlers. The vision was not very bright and I had trouble seeing everything.

October 30, 2004

This vision was quite large. It was from the corner of the room to the curtains. There were three metal chairs. These were outdoor chairs, white but in need of painting.

This vision ruins my theory that the vision appears wherever I'm looking at the time I wake up. I had to turn over to see this one. I also had to turn over to see the "twelve-year-old boy" who was crying. See "Spring, 2003 Boy."

November 1, 2004

The spirits were busy tonight. First, there was a gray and white striped towel, not laid straight but not totally jumbled up, sort of in-between.

Then, there was a window divided into square panes and a tree branch.

Then, the ever-familiar throw: This time right in the middle was a cute line drawing of a kitten with wings. These wings were going very fast, like humming bird's wings.

41

November 10, 2004

Tonight's vision consisted of two or three metal
lawn chairs behind a palm tree. I say two or three
because I could see two, but the scene led me to
believe there was another one hidden by the tree.
This was very amusing or coincidental since the day
before I was thinking that I wouldn't put any more
visions into this document if it were only the brown
throw. All along, I have thought the throw was
covered with fern leaves and now I know that they
were palm leaves. I had also asked the spirits to
make things clearer so that I would know what they
are trying to convey to me.

November 11, 2004

The first vision tonight was a line drawing of a ca-
nary in the palm leaves.

The second was a horse with a bird on its back. The
bird looked like a stuffed animal.

Then there was a dog on an elephant and again
these looked like stuffed animals, kind of comical!

November 19, 2004

Tonight there were two women who were either
Indian or Iraqi. They were wearing full wraps including face and head covers. They were very close
together as if they were whispering to each other.

November 20, 2004

My vision started while Jim and I were still in bed. The light was still out. I looked over to see if Jim was up yet, and that's when I saw a man standing there, right beside Jim's side of the bed. I'm sure it was Jim, and he was rolling up the cuff on his short-sleeved shirt as Jim always does. He was using his left hand to roll up his right sleeve. The vision vanished and Jim got up out of bed right after that.

Something was wrong with this scenario – people are supposed to be dead before they come back in a vision!

I asked a friend of mine who is spiritual and she said it's quite possible. Jim probably doesn't even know he's appearing to me.

November 23, 2004

I saw a lion's head, which looked as if it were on the brown throw. Right beside the lion's head was a pair of handcuffs and something else in silver metal that I did not recognize.

November 24, 2004

Tonight there was a man beside the lion in the middle of the brown throw. His mouth was open in an oval. Perhaps he was singing or at least saying something. He closed his mouth and the vision disappeared.

As I put my pillow back on the bed, I noticed that there was a brown fabric with tiny flowers. This was about the size of a sheet. It was neatly folded. I knew that I couldn't touch it, so I just went back to sleep.

One thing I noticed was that no matter how dark the room was, the visions were all well lighted.

November 25, 2004

Tonight's first vision was the head of a cat and maybe part of the body. I couldn't tell the color since this vision was in black and white.

The second vision of the night was a sweet-looking child. I had to crane my neck so that I could see her because she
was so close to my head. At first, I thought it was Hannah, my great granddaughter, but as I looked closer, I knew it wasn't her. It was a very blonde child, but her teeth weren't like Hannah's. This was a very fleeting vision.

December 1, 2004

There was a man's head on the throw. The throw was over me and the man's head was lying the same way that I was and approximately on my stomach so that I was looking at the top of his head. At first, his eyes were open. Then he blinked a couple of times and left.

December 2, 2004

The brown throw again. This time there was a man's face. He had a thin chinstrap beard and possibly a mustache. He was talking, but I had no audio, and I was looking down at his head, so I couldn't begin to read his lips. He was not smiling and he was moving his lips exaggeratedly as if he were really trying to make me understand. I so wish that I could understand these messages. The brown throw must be very important. I do think it means that I am loved and taken care of.

December 3, 2004

I have three pictures on the south wall of my bedroom, and when I awoke, Jim was dressing in the bathroom with the light on, so the room was very visible. As I looked at that wall, the pictures were all something else besides what I knew them to be.

The farthest to the right was a lion. I don't know if this was just the head or the whole body. The middle one was a beautiful tiger that was looking at me. The farthest one on the left was a lady. She had a dress on, and it looked like double knit fabric. She also had a small scarf tied around her neck such as we wore in the early fifties. She looked very pleasant as far as I could see. I'm nearsighted and that one was hard to focus on.

I am a Leo. Maybe that has something to do with my seeing so many different kinds of cats.

December 4, 2004

My first vision was the black cat I have seen many times. Jim had just slammed his legs down again (he says this helps the constant hurting from his arthritis). The cat walked over his legs and then off the bottom of the bed. Could it be that the reason Jim slammed his legs was that the cat was trying to sleep on them?

The next was a very large portrait of my brother Doug! This is the first one I have recognized absolutely. This picture was huge, about four by six feet. It was an excellent picture of him. He had his foot propped up on something, and he was leaning on his knee with his forearm. He was smiling.

The next went back a few months. There were palm leaves on a window (it may be that the leaves were on a tree on the outside of the window). Through the window, there was the plastic outdoor chair that I have seen several times, floating down into the picture.

December 5, 2004

There was a huge ape head in the middle of the picture. When I looked at part of his body, his skin was the same design that is very familiar to me – the brown throw.

There was a fast vision of a lady with a large-brimmed hat. This vision was all in white, so I couldn't make out any details of her face.

46

Sometimes it seems that a lot of people, animals, and things are trying to contact me all at the same time.

December 6, 2004

Sometime during the night, I woke up and I was standing looking over the back of my chair.   There was a woman sitting in my rocker. She was reading. All I could see was one of her shoulders, arm, and both hands.

The second vision looked like the whole wall was a trellis covered by ivy. As I watched, the entire trellis and ivy moved close to the bed and stopped just before it touched the bed on Jim's side. I believe Jim was already up.

December 11, 2004

When I first opened my eyes, I was facing "Jim." He was rubbing his finger beside his nose and wearing stripped pajamas. I looked farther and saw that Jim was already up and in the shower. Besides, he doesn't wear striped pajamas.

December 16, 2004

I was looking at the pictures on the bedroom wall. One of the pictures had the frame wrapped very poorly with red yarn. In the next picture to the right, the things were outlined in the red yarn (very good job).

A picture of a sixties typewriter; I'm sure I used one just like this. It could have been one of my dad's.

December 17, 2004

This night on the wall I saw three women's outfits on the wall that suddenly started struggling to get away from the wall.

Tonight's second vision: Jim was coming out of the bathroom, ready for work. He always kisses me before he leaves. As I looked at him, I saw him begin to hurry over to the bed. I turned over and "he" was standing beside me very close and moved toward me as if he might kiss me. I said, "What are you doing?" because at that moment I knew it was a vision. It was very slow to recede.

The third vision was a hand, palm up. It looked like a plaster cast of a large hand.

December 22, 2004

This vision was rather out of character with the visions of the last month. I saw a woman with blond, short, curly hair sitting in a car. She was wrapped in the brown throw. I was looking from behind her right shoulder. She seemed as if she were getting ready to get out of the car. The vision ended before she made any move.

December 28, 2004

The first vision tonight was the lion's head in the

middle of the brown throw and it was larger than usual. When I opened my eyes and saw it, it smiled and gave me the long slow blinks that mean love to cats.

The second vision tonight was a rectangular box. It looked as if it contained something electrical. There was a plug-in cord attached to the bottom. The cord was white;
the box was white on all sides except the middle where it was tan. The cord was tied up with a twist tie. It looked like a new item.

December 29, 2004

Tonight I was looking at a bed with the bedspread pulled off the bottom of the mattress.

December 30, 2004

The brown throw had the lion again, but this time he was yawning.

December 31, 2004

It was almost dinnertime, 5:00 p.m., and I was in the living room and Jim had just walked out to the kitchen to stir the soup. I heard a cat chortle, and I said, "What do you want, Sabrina? Do you want out?" When Jim came back into the living room, he asked, "With whom were you talking?" I said, "Sabrina." He said Sabrina was asleep in her cat tree. I guess my very vocal vision-cat is even here in the daytime.

January 1, 2005

I thought I'd do an experiment so I asked my angel helper, "Victor", to send me something different. I guess I got what I asked for.

The vision was a little Mickey Mouse about three inches tall. It was moving its right hand. At least Victor has a sense of humor.

January 2 2005

I saw an American flag in a window. It looked as if it were stuck to the window like contact paper.

January 3, 2005

This vision was two hands; right and left, holding a red cloth about twelve to fifteen inches long. The hands were backside up as if playing one potato, two potato.

January 4, 2005

This was a vision of a man's face. I thought of Martin Luther King.

January 5, 2005

This was a quick side view of a man's face. It was long and slender. If I had had more time to look at it, I would have said it was handsome. This viewing seemed to me as if it didn't entirely come through to me.

50

January 6, 2005

There was a quilt draped over a chair. I think the chair was an outdoor plastic chair with arms. It floated to the right, and when the bottom of the quilt went past the headboard of the bed, it wrinkled. This substantiates my idea that people cannot touch the visions, but inanimate objects can.

This vision was two hands playing poker. The right hand held a cigarette between his fingers. There were poker chips on the table.

January 8, 2005

This vision was just a white teddy bear. There was something colorful, but it lasted such a short period of time that I don't remember what was colorful.

January 9, 2005

What I saw tonight was the bottom half of a stair-way. It was made up of a dark varnished handrail and very fancy end post. The small posts were painted white. It looked very nice.

January 10, 2005

This was dog night! The first vision was a cross between a bloodhound and a yellow lab. The back half of him was sitting on a chair and his front legs were on the floor.

The next was a yellow lab, sitting the same way.

Then there was a golden retriever sitting the same way. All were very cute and looked friendly.

I'm behind a lady who was wearing a green blazer with pinkish roses on it. She was sitting at a desk and working with a computer.

This was a white eyelet curtain hanging right where my curtains hang in the bedroom, but mine are lace, not eyelet. Below the tieback, there was movement as if something were trying to get out from inside the curtain. It never made it while I was watching.

January 11, 2005

I have had the same vision twice. I wasn't going to put any more of this type in this document, but since they sent it to me twice, I thought I'd better document it.

There were two heads. One of the heads was left of center and was a lion; the other was lower and right of center.

This one was a monkey or an ape of some kind. Both animals were moving their mouths.

January 13, 2005

This was a medium blue and white horizontal striped golf shirt. I'm hoping that it is Dad trying to contact me, or just saying "Hi." He was a professional golfer.

January 14, 2005

The phone rang and Jim answered it. I wanted to go back to sleep, so I closed my eyes. Then it dawned on me that Jim wasn't getting up, so I opened my eyes and saw Jim lying in bed as he had been except his chest was uncovered, and he was holding his hands above his chest with the finger-tips touching. I thought he was deciding whether he really wanted to go exercise or not. Just then he got up and vanished! Then I heard the shower start running. Jim had already been in the bathroom for about ten minutes. I still don't know how a live person can send his spirit, but the psychic says he can. She said he usually is unaware of it.

January 15, 2005

I saw "Jim" get up and come around the bed. Actually, Jim was just getting up at this point. In other words, these things were happening simultaneously. The apparition was wearing a flannel cotton shirt. I believe it was white. He came very close to me and leaned over and kissed me on the forehead. I did not feel this, but I just knew it.

January 20, 2005

The first vision tonight was a large rabbit hand puppet. He was either standing on Jim's stomach or just beside it.

The second was two hand puppets hugging. These had little round ears, so I assumed that they might have been little bears. I saw only the back of them, and there wasn't any particular color.

January 23, 2005

This vision was a side view of a man standing on Jim's side of the bed. He had on a red plaid shirt. I thought this may be Dad, but he wouldn't be wearing a plaid shirt.

When I opened my eyes, an eye was staring right at my eye. As I kept looking, the eye was backing away and turned into a face. It was a man's face, which I had seen before, but I don't know who it is.

The brown throw was back! There was a lion or tiger in the middle with his teeth showing. It didn't really look mad, but I guess I'd say it looked fierce.

February 2, 2005

There was a large built tall man standing by the bed on my side. He was holding a baby doll on his left shoulder. His hair was gray and he wore a wedding ring.

February 4, 2005

A lady was lying beside me on the outside of the mattress. Her hair looked artificial, as if it were molded and painted.

The next vision showed me that the brown throw was back, but this time, it had a lion's head from the

54

back. Maybe that meant he was turning his back on me. Down to my right was a darling kitten.

The last vision tonight was a gym bag with a girl's face hanging upside down from it.

February 5, 2005

There was a fireman holding a white pitcher. This pitcher was the old-fashioned type used in bedrooms where there was no bathroom upstairs or perhaps inside.

February 6, 2005
I was awake in the middle of the night and couldn't go back to sleep. I thought I might as well pray, and while I was doing this, a loud "meow" interrupted me. Our cat sleeps in the garage, so it wasn't her.

February 7, 2005

This night's first vision was a white T-shirt with a round collar. As I watched, the left sleeve moved as if something were inside.

The second vision for tonight was a body lying on a gurney-type table. It was covered up.

The third thing that happened tonight took place when I got up in the middle of the night to go to the bathroom, and as I got to the side of the bed, I noticed that we were both covered up by the brown throw. I thought that was kind of cute and thoughtful. I guess the spirits have finally accepted Jim.

February 9, 2005

This vision was of a large glass "flask." It was made of swirled glass with a bulbous base. It had a cork in the top.

This was sitting on the brown throw that was covering (probably) a chest of drawers.

February 11, 2005 to March 30, 2005

My computer crashed so I recreated these visions at a later time and that's why there are no dates on the following:

Tonight's vision was a blue windbreaker-type jacket with a crest on the upper front left. It was hanging on a hanger.

Later this same night, it was the brown throw with a male lion in the center. There was a female lion off to the side.

This night, there was a bookcase that covered the entire wall. It was painted green.

This was a stone lion that twitched his nose as if he were going to sneeze. He also moved his eyes.

There was a long-stem rose in the middle of the throw. Again, it may be conveying love.

This time, there was a house cat in the middle of the throw. Later that night we were covered up with the
56

throw.

A man in a white cap and gown was moving and shaking his finger at me.

At bedtime, I had prayed that I would know some of the people I am seeing, expecting that they would have already passed over. Later that night I awoke to see a woman standing by me, and she finally bent over me and kissed me on the lips. (I could not feel the kiss.) Then she straightened up. I smiled at her and she smiled back. She looked like Barb Hemry and she is very much alive. Barb is my brother, Phil's, wife. We are not very close, but we are friendly and talk a lot when we are together. They also live in Springfield, Ohio, which is about a three-hour drive from our house. [note: Barb died of cancer about five months after this sighting.]

There was an oval face with a dark tan very close to my head. It had many wrinkles that ran around his head in ovals. Scary looking! He moved his mouth and blinked his eyes.

There were two hands with their fingers straight out.

There was a man's face very close to Jim's. He wore a red knit hat. He had a very long face with protruding chin.

Before I got up, I saw a white dove over by the doorway to the hall. I thought that if I got near it, it would disappear. I got up and walked right past it on my way to the bathroom. It did not vanish.

This was a pig's head. He blinked his eyes.

The brown throw was back and there were animal faces next to it.

One of the bedroom walls was decorated for Halloween.

A fist was under the chin propping up a person's head. This reminded me of a pose for a portrait.

I think someone knows how much I like to bake. Anyway, this vision was a file drawer full of baking pans.

This was the usual brown throw with a normal lion's head.

Sometimes visions are just funny. What I saw was a wooden plaque in the shape of a shield with a sleepy lion and a skeleton head. The skeleton scratched his ear with his foot.

It's a very common vision, but it's bound to mean something. The brown throw was back with a normal lion in the middle.

The next night I saw a huge buffalo with a head on each end.

Things don't seem to be telling me anything in any logical time frame. But I know I'll know what everyone of them means when I cross over. This was a dark pink satin spread, which was being held up

58

so that I could see the whole thing. It was at the end of our bed.

The computer is fixed, but the spirits were really busy while it was broken.

March 31, 2005

This was the same throw, but I was seeing the other side of it, so it was a white background with brown lines. There was a sailboat on it.
.
April 1, 2005

At 5:49 a.m., I awoke thinking that Jim was coming into the room to kiss me goodbye before he left for work. As he got closer, I noted that he did not have his uniform on. At this point, I knew it was a vision. He had on a white shirt and pants or a white jump suit. As he neared my side of the bed, he began to float over me, and when he got in the right place, he put out his hand as if to touch my face. While he was coming around the bed, I understood him to say "check on her, check on her." I know it was Jim. When he came home, I asked him where he was at 5:49 a.m. and he said in New Boston on his way to work. This is the third time Jim has appeared to me.

April 5, 2005

Tonight I saw a small wrinkled old woman with no teeth, chewing.

April 6, 2005

"Jim" was by his side of the bed and he was bobbing his head and upper body up and down very slowly. I watched him several times; then I asked, "What are you doing?" Jim, who was lying beside me, asked, "What did you say?" It was then that I knew it was a vision.

I awoke to see a small lady standing very close to me. She was pretty old, but I don't remember or saw whether she had many wrinkles. She was just looking at me. I don't know if it was the same lady that I had seen before or not. She was standing so close and closer to the top of my head, so I had to crane my neck to see her. When I did, she slowly disappeared.

April 10, 2005

As I awoke, there was a small dark gray bird up next to the ceiling over our bed. He was moving his little wings like a helicopter.

April 11, 2005

Here was the same little bird, but he landed on the picture over the bed. I had to get up on one elbow to see him over the top of the headboard.

April 20, 2005

This vision was of four toys made of metal like when I was a child. The only one I can remember
60

was an airplane. I didn't write this one down as soon as it was over. I didn't think it was important, but who is to say what this was meant to convey to me?

April 21, 2005

My mother was in a bed next to my side of our bed, but it was several feet above my bed. She appeared to be sleeping. She was lying on her right side with her left arm over her head. She moved as if to get more comfortable, and when she did, her breasts protruded from the top of her nightgown. I believe she showed me this so that I could see that she had been given a new body in Heaven. She now had two breasts. Mother died of breast cancer in 1979 after having one breast completely removed. This was such a blessing for me to see because the surgeons had so mutilated her body. I don't have to guess what this vision meant!

April 27, 2005

Tonight's vision was of another toy. This was a jack-in-the-box made of metal. It had a picture of Uncle Sam on the sides, and this was in bright red, white, and blue. This was probably made sometime in the 1940's.

April 28, 2005

Jim and I were asleep until I awoke and saw a large yellow and white, longhaired cat lying almost head-high between Jim and me. We did have a yellow cat a long time ago, but he died very young. I don't know if he had any white on him or not.

April 29, 2005

I have had many sightings of the brown throw. I haven't included them in here because they were so ordinary. But tonight, we were, again, covered up with the throw. In the middle of the throw, was the usual lion, but he was moving his lips as if he were talking or maybe trying to get me to understand something. Of course, I didn't get his meaning at all. I surely wish I could have. It might have un-locked the secret to this throw.

April 30, 2005

Tonight's vision was a short-sleeved jean jacket over a short-sleeved red plaid shirt. I somehow knew that this was a child. All I could see was the left sleeve because it seemed as though the rest of her was under my head. I say female because this was the feeling I had.

This was a quick vision, but still a vision. It was a silver phone and three remote controls.

May 4, 2005

I don't know what they are trying to tell me. This vision was two coffee carafes and two lanterns.

May 8, 2005

Tonight, I saw a curtain (one half of a pair) made of plaid, blue and white flannel. The background was white with blue stripes. It was moving as if someone were behind it and trying to get out. This is the second or third time I've seen something like this. Who would make curtains out of plaid flannel?

May 11, 2005

This vision was a ten to twelve-year-old boy with very blond hair bowing his head over Jim. I say bowing, but not necessarily praying. He was next to Jim's head and shoulder. Jim's eyes were open. When I later asked Jim if he saw the boy, he said that he hadn't seen anything.

Another vision the same night! This was the ever-recurring brown throw with the Zulu mask. He was smiling very big this time.

May 12, 2005

This was a fist full of dollars. The hand was holding a bunch of bills that were fanned out. I was hoping this meant we were probably going to get some money.

June 2, 2005

I didn't record this vision very soon after I had it, so I've forgotten most of the details. This was a young man covered with the throw. I'm not sure of the date I had this vision.

Another in the same night was an old man (my age) in bed. He lifted his head, looked at me, and smiled. He was an attractive man, and I believe he had a white mustache. At first I thought I was seeing the picture in the frame hanging on the wall where I was looking, so to test it I moved my eyes, and the image moved with me. Obviously, this was not a dark impression of the picture that is of a winter scene.

June 6, 2005

This was a vision of a rather handsome young man changing a baby's diaper. All I could see of the baby were its legs kicking.

June 7, 2005

This was just a group of several office machines, all gray, all pushed together. There was a computer tower, and that's all I can remember since I let this go for several days without documenting it. (I wasn't going to put this sighting into this document because it was so different and I couldn't see the sense in it. But the next day I got a tip on a new job.)

June 8, 2005

This vision was of a tiger in the middle of the brown throw. All he did was close his eyes very slowly. Now, if he were a domestic cat, this is the sign of love. Maybe that's what he was telling me too.

June 9, 2005

Here's another strange one! This was a football helmet that was decorated in red, white, and blue stripes. The face guard was going up and down. Maybe God likes football, too?

June 10, 2005

This takes place in the top of a closet. There were blankets, and one of them was wiggling as if something were pushing it off the shelf from the back. I blinked my eyes and the blanket was gone. There on the shelf was an angel lamp with a tiny man standing beside the lamp and pointing with both hands to the lamp. He was dressed in a tuxedo and white gloves. I thought this was cute and really hilarious since I had asked my angel guides to help the messages become more clear to me since I don't know what so many of them mean. This one was quite clear. It told me that the angels are with me, and I believe the lamp was representing the light bulb being the light bulb of recognition – in other words... Duh! (This is something my great-grandchildren say when I say something obvious.)

June 15, 2005

I wasn't going to write any more of my visions because I am so disturbed by the people who don't believe me. I want to talk about these happenings and I can't find many people with whom I can broach this subject. This includes many very religious people. What are they praying for if it's not everlasting life? My visions have decreased in number, I think, because I'm upset about the feelings of other people. Anyway, tonight was the throw except it was green and yellow. The lion's head had the throw pulled up to his neck, and in the lower right corner was the head of the monkey that I have seen before.

June 29, 2005

There was a woman looking up as if she were praying. There was a baby in the background lying on the throw. The baby looked chubby and healthy. The woman appeared to be about thirty years old.

June 30, 2005

This vision was a lion's head with a profuse mane. It was gray and I thought it might be made of concrete. He was moving his mouth and trying very hard to communicate with me.

My visions seem to be getting fewer and farther apart. I hope they don't stop. I look forward to them so much.

I'm sure they are messages from the other side. If I only knew what the messages were!

July 9, 2005

This was the first vision I'd had for a while. It was a woman, I'd say in her thirties, who was wearing a cotton, well-ironed dress with cap sleeves. The sleeves were adorned with a button, I think. Her head and arms were above a bookcase. She seemed to be arguing with someone. As usual, I didn't recognize her.

July 12, 2005

What I saw this night was a doll floating over me that turned into a real baby.

July 14, 2005

I guess I didn't get the message from the other night. This vision was a snowman floating over me. He didn't change into anything.

July 17, 2005

I was working on the computer in our home office and I smelled cigarette smoke. I wondered if it could be one of my family coming for a "visit." I went to a psychic several days later, and she said it was my dad and that he is around me all the time.

July 23, 2005

Tonight was the brown throw hanging on the wall, and while I watched, a red-orange flower bloomed in the center of it. This was shown to me on the inside of my eyelids, and when I opened my eyes to see, it was on the wall. I saw it only a second; then it went away.

July 31, 2005

I was watching TV in the living room tonight, and it changed channels all by itself!

August 3, 2005

This vision was a wrought-iron sculpture of trees and houses. As if I were looking at a very quiet inviting neighborhood.

August 4, 2005

There was a chimp with a brown and red plaid scarf around his neck. His head was up, but then he laid it over as if to go to sleep. I had the impression that a person was holding him although I couldn't see anyone. He may have been a baby chimp, but not a newborn.

August 6, 2005

I think this was a guitar case although it was thicker and shaped a bit differently. Behind it was a person, perhaps Chinese, with a domed paper hat. Maybe this was a case for a Chinese instrument that I don't know about.

August 7, 2005

This was a fun vision! There was the head of a woman, maybe in her thirties, I really couldn't tell, and, she was smiling and had her tongue stuck out at me. I do believe that this was my Ohio State

68

University roommate, Judy Yost Chubbuck who died at about sixty years of age of breast cancer.

August 15, 2005

Several weeks ago, I had a psychic reading by Hazel in Portsmouth, Ohio. She said my dad was speaking through her, and he said, "You know all the things you've misplaced and then find?" "That's me!" I had received two very important documents having to do with our cruise the next month. I had to have them because they told us exactly what we had to do before boarding the ship. I looked high and low for these things. I spent two entire days tearing our house apart, trying to find them. Last night, the last night before we were to leave for the plane, after I had said my prayers, I thought, I'm going to ask Dad to help me find them, or better yet, where he had hidden the documents. The answer came immediately—I got out of bed and went straight to where the booklets were "hiding." They were in the cabinets above our computer where Jim keeps his compact discs and other things he needs to run the computer. I would never have put them in there.

August 16, 2005

The vision tonight was my ever-present brown throw. Actually, this scenario has appeared several times. In the middle of the throw, there was a flower like a chrysanthemum, but it was the one with the spider-like petals instead of the flat ones, and this flower was moving as if in time exposures of plant growth. The flower was orange and green. (The orange may have been closer to red.) Although the action was in the middle of the throw, the first thing I saw was individual fish among the palm fronds—no movement.

August 17, 2005

Tonight's vision was a very fast one. There was a large red bow with long tails in the upper left hand corner of the picture that IS actually hanging there. It was somewhat like the pictures that they wrap and put bows on at Christmas time.

August 19, 2005

Last night's vision started with a hand, palm down. Then it started to move, and it ended up in the wave position—palm facing out. Then the little finger on that hand bent to a permanently bent finger. I knew immediately who was trying to come through—my great uncle Walter Moulton. He had a permanently bent little finger that all of us kids tried to straighten out. I don't know what caused this. Walt was totally blind, but I believe the reason he showed me the bent finger was that I was so intent on straightening it. I finally got the chance to tell him that I was sorry for not visiting him more when he moved into the nursing home.

August 26, 2005

It's been several nights between visions, so I was glad to see this one. Jim had to get up at 5:30 a.m.

this morning so the bathroom light was on but the door was closed. I had been awake since about 3:00 a.m. I rolled over to try to go back to sleep when on the wall appeared a small square of wrought-iron fencing. Then it started to spread until most of that wall was covered. Up in the far left-hand corner was a picture frame with the picture of a man. It was very dark and almost out of my vision, but I thought if it were closer to me that I may have recognized him. He was moving and "talking" as if he were trying to communicate with me. Of course, I heard nothing. Maybe he'll come back.

September 2, 2005

Jim was in the bathroom with the light on early this morning when I got the vision of another outdoor metal chair. It had a unique design for the back and was painted white. This vision was another one that was imprinted on the insides of my eyelids. When I slowly opened one of my eyes, the chair started to fade; when I opened the other eye, it vanished. One thing I have noticed about most of these visions is that when they start to vanish or fade, they sort of float to the upper right or left of my sight area.

September 4, 2005

I had a short vision tonight. It was a man inside a frame, life size. He was huge built and had on a work shirt. He had a full mustache that covered his lip. When I saw this vision, it frightened me, so I got rid of it fast by blinking my eyes. Now I wish I had watched him a while longer. He wasn't smiling. He was looking very serious.

September 12, 2005

The alarm had just gone off, and I rolled up to see if Jim had gotten up yet. He hadn't. Right beside and at right angles to his face was another face. It looked a lot like Jim but had more wrinkles. Then Jim got up and the vision disappeared. The background for this was the brown throw.

September 14, 2005

This vision was a little girl's ruffled, eyelet dress, but right in the middle (at waist level) was a clown doll (stuffed, I think). Also, this dress was in an adult size.

October 8, 2005

This vision was of a man and woman sitting on a bench wrapped in throws.

The next vision tonight looked like a leg with a full stocking on and a pair of running shoes and everything was in blue. This was probably someone's leg dressed for a ballgame.

October 15, 2005

I'm not having very many visions now, but the brown throw has come through several times. The lion in the middle has been getting larger.

72

October 30, 2005

There was a man's head in the picture frame in our bedroom. I thought, was hoping really, that it was Dad, but when it came into better view, it wasn't. He had a cigarette dangling from the side of his mouth. His eyes were slanted and his head was triangular. He had a tear in his eye.

I wish I knew what I am supposed to learn from all of this!

November 1, 2005

I wasn't going to include this in this document because I really don't know if I was dreaming or awake. All the books that I have read on the subject say that these visions can come to you through a dream.

I saw a paperback book, the size of a magazine. The cover was heavier than a usual magazine, more like a paperback novel. The cover was a caramel color with a late middle-aged woman with gray hair walking on a road or street. There was nothing to tell me if it was a city street or country road. The name of this pamphlet was "When Last Tolls Life". This pamphlet was probably forty to fifty pages long. I looked the title up on the computer and it was not there.

November 6, 2005

Ugh! Another sleepless night! I went to sleep about

11:30 p.m. and woke about 2:30 a.m. I lay there for hours. At last, I thought, as long as I'm awake anyway, I may as well be seeing visions. So I asked the spirits or whoever was in charge of this sort of thing to send me a vision. I tossed and turned some more. I kept opening my eyes just to check to see if any vision was in sight, but there wasn't. I reached up to put my pillow down so that I could lie on my back for a while, and there on the bookcase headboard was a small animal statue. I thought at first that it was a mule, but the more I looked at it, the more I decided it was the head of a camel with a mule's body. Anyway, he was comical looking. The more I thought about it, the more I felt that this was the camel from the pack of cigarettes called Camels. I feel sure that this was Dad's doing again. I am so pleased that he is responding to my wishes. Maybe some day he will come through visually to me.

November 11, 2005

I awoke to see a statue of an eagle standing next to the head of Jim's side of the bed. It had its wings folded against its sides. He was gray. It looked like a wooden carving having been done with a chain saw. I think his neck feathers were white. He was not illuminated very well.

November 13, 2005

I knew it was early morning, but I wanted to see if it were light yet, so I opened one eye and saw the brown throw covering us again. It's nice to be loved.

November 15, 2005

There was a lady's head to my upper left. She had
shoulder-length gray hair. As I watched, she aged
many years.

November 28, 2005

This vision was of an orchid that was blowing very
gently in the wind. A fairy was dancing very close
to the orchid. Very short vision but pleasant.

November 29, 2005

This vision was like a fast movie or maybe like
watching scenery from a moving car window with
the film speeded up. Anyway, I'm almost sure this
was Dad. Dad was a professional golfer. It started
by my seeing a golf course and then zoomed into a
golfer with the club in the follow through position,
as if he had just hit the ball. Again, this view was as
if I were on the ground looking up at a man's face.
The short glimpse I had, I really think it was Dad.
I want to communicate with him so badly. Maybe
I just assigned his face to these visions. *(A funny
thing happened while I was writing this – our door-
bell rang. When I went to answer it, no one was in
sight!)*

December 6, 2005

I was still in bed and half awake. Jim was in the

bathroom. He came into the bedroom to get dressed, and I opened one eye. There was a little hand trying to wiggle back under the covers on Jim's side.

January 2, 2006

There was a "being," a cross between an ape and a man, and he was straightening or tucking in the covers around Jim's hips.

January 4, 2006

There was a cat tree. I don't believe it was ours. There were stuffed monkey toys hanging by one arm all over the tree.

January 6, 2006

The brown throw was there with a man's face in the middle. He aged as I watched and got very old with many wrinkles. Is God trying to tell me something?

I had decided not to write any more of these, but since last night was so interesting I decided I'd document it.

March 9, 2006

Yesterday I was so lonely that I couldn't think straight. I went to a Lenten service and prayed to God to lead my life.

The first vision He sent me was the brown throw

76

with a "Blue Bird of Happiness" in flight on it.

The second was a "teddy bear" made from the throw.

These visions sent the message loud and clear that God knows how unhappy I am and that I am surrounded by love and warmth.

March 12, 2006

Tonight's first vision was a plastic-type lawn chair with no arms. It was tipped over. This happened to another lawn chair much earlier in my vision history only the first one had arms. I don't have any idea what these could be telling me other than possibly the death of someone.

This second vision happened immediately after the first. It was a gravesite with earth mounded as if it were a new grave. It had a headstone, but it looked like the old-style marble ones.

This second vision happened immediately after the first. It was a gravesite with earth mounded as if it were a new grave. It had a headstone, but it looked like the old-style marble ones.

May 13, 2006

I was sleeping on my stomach when I felt something touch my arm. The covers were between Jim and I. When I moved my arm, there was nothing there. At first I thought it was Sabrina, our cat, but she rarely sleeps with us, and when she does, she sleeps down by my legs.

May 14, 2006

As I opened my eyes in the middle of the night, I was staring right into the eyes of Tom, one of the cats we'd had when we lived at the 100 Mile House. The vet had to put him to sleep about two years ago because he had feline aids.

The visions left me for no reason I can see for 4 years then inexplicably returned.

July 10, 2010

Jim was working today, so it was just Sabrina, our cat, in the house with me. I was doing some house-work and I wanted to put away some of the clothes that I had just washed and folded. I walked from the living room, past the front room where Sabrina was sitting by the windows. I picked up the folded clothes and started walking to our bedroom. "The cat" zoomed right past me using her "elephant walk." As I walked back into the living room, past the front room, Sabrina was still sitting in front of the windows!

August 31, 2010

I awoke sometime in the middle of the night need-ing to use the bathroom. I'm very careful when I get up at night because it's pretty dark in our bed-room, and the dog sleeps in there with us. As I got

78

out of bed, I spotted "Boone" lying under the windows. (It's cooler there and he has very long hair.) So I started for the bathroom without being very careful because I already knew where Boone was. As I approached the bathroom, I tripped over Boone and fell flat on my face. I broke my nose. When I finally got to the point where I could get up and think I realized that the "Boone" under the window was a vision. The real Boone was quite surprised when I tripped over him. Fortunately, he wasn't hurt.

October 6, 2011

At 7:00 a.m. the phone rang for our "wake up" call, but it rang only once and it was obvious that Jim hadn't heard it. So I said "Jim," waited a few seconds, and said it again. I did this several times and he did not respond. I instantly thought something was wrong because he was lying on his back next to me. (I could see him – he was covered up to his neck, but he was very surely asleep, and I could even see his flat-top haircut.) I decided to pat him. That didn't work either. I got up on one elbow and decided I'd shake him. When I tried that, the blanket went flat and the vision disappeared. Jim was already in the bathroom!

October 7, 2011

Tonight it was two ironing boards. These were about half the length of a real ironing board and one was all red and the other was about one third red.

Then the brown throw was there again, and in the middle was a tiger's face with green eyes. A small pumpkin was just beside the tiger.

The last vision was a Trojan-type soldier carved into a large, heavy piece of wood – probably a double door that you would see in a very old castle or church.

October 8, 2011

I awoke to see a black "bird" with small round white spots on his body. His wings were flapping extremely fast, and he seemed to have several on each side of his body. He was flying very slowly away from me and up toward the ceiling. When he had almost reached the ceiling, he vanished. It then dawned on me that it wasn't a bird, but a Black Molly fish. Could this have been a sign that I wasn't going to have any more visions?

October 10, 2011

This vision was of a plastic or metal outdoor chair; different from the ones I have seen before. The brown throw was draped over the seat and down to the floor. It may have been representing someone who was sitting outside in this chair and whose legs were covered with the throw, and then the person left.

October 11, 2011

What a surprise! Our cat Sabrina died in July of

this year. I was in the kitchen getting things out to fix dinner when here comes Sabrina "walking" over to me. She looked up as if to say, "What are you fixing?" I was looking directly down on her, so it looked as if she were walking on the floor. Her legs were moving as if she were walking, but I know she wasn't. She disappeared as fast as she had come. It was so good to see her again.

October 12, 2011

The first vision was like an X-ray picture of the back of the head. It clearly showed the spine.
.
The second was a large head and face of a man with a beard. The eyes slowly closed and opened.

The third was a woman standing over (behind) a boy, probably nine or ten years old. The faces were neutral and reminded me of a teacher and student.

I was cold and couldn't go to sleep. After lying there for several hours I thought I'd open my eyes just to check if anything was there. There was a light green golf bag full of clubs!

I finally went to sleep between 2:00 and 3:00 a.m. but kept waking up because I was so cold. This time when I woke up, I was toasty warm. I looked down at the cover, and it was the brown throw covering both of us. I smiled and it went away. I was warm until I got up at 8:00 a.m. I asked Jim if he had been cold last night, and he said, "Yes" but that he had felt warm right after that.

It was time for me to get up, and when I opened my eyes, there were two green broad pencil-line drawings of horses, and they were galloping across the wall.

October 13, 2011

The lion's head on the brown throw was looking at me and he began blinking his eyes at me very slowly. To cats, this is the sign they use to say, "I love you". All day long I thought that maybe that was the last time these visions would visit me.

October 14, 2011

This vision was very interesting. As I opened my eyes, there was a slender woman probably in her late fifties, standing close to my side of the bed. She extended her arms and unfolded the greenish-gray blanket she was holding. Then she bent forward and acted as if she were covering maybe a child that was lying next to me. This was a very bright, strong vision and it took quite a while for her to fade away.

October 15, 2011

I awoke looking straight into the eyes of a medium-to-long-haired cat. When he was sure that I saw him, he turned his head as if going to go to sleep. He was all gray with a lightening-type mark down his side. I could see only one side.

October 16, 2011

The first vision of the night was a metal lunch box – the kind kids carry although I never had one. It had a picture on it, but I couldn't make out what it was.

Next there was a large red cat face. It was just there.

Then there was a puppet on strings. It was dancing around. This was a crazy night! A pack of cigarettes flashed on the wall and was gone before I could read the brand name.

Next there was a space heater that just stood there.

Then there was a green ladder that had about four steps, which hopped and walked all over the place. *Things like this make this experience fun and I look forward to them.*

The best thing was the brown throw. It had the palm leaf pattern on it again. When I put my pillow down, there it was all folded up on the bookcase part of the bed. I tried to see if I could touch it, and my hand went right through it, but my pillow didn't. I wasn't surprised about not being able to touch it, but I was surprised that the pillow touched it.

October 17, 2011

This night was a jumble of things. The ever-popular throw was there except that it was showing its white side. This was hung over a wall lamp, and there

was a man's face, or mask, that had his mouth open
in an oval. Then there was a football and that's all
I can remember. The throw looked as though it
had a jumble of lines on it but not the familiar palm
fronds.

October 18, 2011 Movie time.

This one started sometime early in the evening.
Jim hadn't come into the bedroom yet, so the lights
were still on. There appeared a frame about three
by four feet. This was showing me a bicycle that
seemed to be in an enclosed room. It was in black
and white, so I couldn't tell the color. I assumed
this was my bike when I lived at home and it should
have been blue. I couldn't see if it had a bar or
not. It was lying on its side. I figured it was in the
garage with the door closed.

From there the "screen" began to move farther
away, and it turned into a toddler running away.
The screen was fast moving away and getting dim-
mer. This happened on the east wall of the bedroom
and started about three inches down from the top of
the wall. This toddler reminded me of my brother,
Phillip. I couldn't see his hair close enough to see
if it indeed could have been blond curly hair like
Phil's, but the body reminded me of him. The screen
disappeared at the top of the wall.

November 21, 2011 The Angels' Visit

Cherry, our daughter, sent me an e-mail and asked me if I would like to host five archangels (Michael, Gabriel, Raphael, Uriel, and Metatron) for five evenings. Since I am writing a spiritual book, I thought this would be wonderful. She said they would arrive at 10:30 p.m. on December 2, 2011.

I was to set up a small altar, which included a white candle, a white flower, and a sealed envelope with three questions and an apple for me to eat after they leave on the fifth evening.

When it was 10:30 p.m. on December 2, I opened the front door and welcomed them. I sat in a comfortable chair and meditated. I also asked questions each evening. The directions also said that I might wake up between 3 and 5a.m. with insights and guidance.

Among the many questions I asked were: 1) Will I get cancer again? 2) Will my visions return? These are the questions I felt I received answers to.

During my first meditation of the archangels' visit one of the names I heard was Hannah. Five days later, on December 7, 2011, Vicki, my daughter-in-law called me and said my great-granddaughter, Hannah, had won third place in her school's science fair. She had done an experiment on the effectiveness of hand sanitizers versus washing with soap.

The odd thing about this is several years ago, when

I was helping a third-grade teacher at what is now Hannah's school; I did the same science experiment with that class. This took place several weeks before Debbie told me she was expecting a baby, which turned out to be Hannah. *No one in the family knew about my teaching this experiment to this class.*

The first night of the archangel's visit I was awakened at 4:50 a.m. and a silent voice said to me, "We are going to a place you wouldn't want to go." This was the quote from the archangels.

On the second night of the archangels' visit I had this dream. I seemed to be in a foreign country watching some children playing a game that I didn't know. They had some sort of crooked bat (maybe a tree branch) and something that wasn't round like a ball. I didn't get a good look at that. Right next to where they were playing was a small pond with an alligator and several medium-size snakes. Other people were on the deck with me watching these animals. We were not afraid of them. We were seeing the beauty in them.

On the third night while I was meditating, Opal, my husband's deceased mother, came to mind. My hand started to tingle. I told Opal if she were here, I would like her to try to move the candle flame so that I would know for sure that it was really she. I had been amazed that this candle burned so straight. It never wavered at all by itself. So after a few minutes, the candle flame did begin to wave slightly. I told Opal that she was a strong woman, and I knew that she could make this candle move more than that. Well, I could hardly believe this, but that flame jumped all over the place. The furnace was not on and there was no other movement in the room. *(The only other time I saw any movement in this flame was when I disturbed the air by putting my notebook down quickly.)*

On the third night, at 3:19 a.m., I was awakened and this is the vision that came through:

I went to a building where a doctor was interacting with many patients. This was a large room. Most of the people were mentally handicapped. One young man had his hands and lower part of his arms and both lower legs gone. He was using some special equipment. A mentally challenged group was drinking coffee and eating cookies, one man was painting. He kept starting new paintings, but the one he had finished was of a beautiful room in a house, and through this room you could see the kitchen. The kitchen had several live black and white cows standing in it. It was a wonderful picture, and who would have thought of putting such humor into a beautiful picture? I was smiling in my half sleep.

I was there to see the doctor for my upper back. I lay on several beds and tables, and the doctor felt my back and talked to me. He gave me a cup of coffee, which tasted like nothing I recognized, but it was delicious. Then he gave me a package of two cookies, and one of the mentally challenged women said, "Only one, only one!" But I think I ate them both. They were wonderful, and they also had a taste I didn't recognize. I got the impression that the doctor wanted me to lose weight. I asked him where I could get some more of these cookies, and he reached to the top of something like a refrigerator and gave me a whole box of them.

On the fourth night, I slept soundly and without interruption.

On the fifth night, at 4:07a.m. I woke to a very clear scene.

I was getting chemo. I assume I got my answer to the question about getting cancer again.

December 8, 2011

I was just returning home from my exercise class, and as I opened the door from the garage to the kitchen, I saw a very slender man hurrying from the kitchen to the dining room. It was as if he didn't want me to see him. He was dressed in the 1940's style. He wore black pants, gray vest, and a white shirt. I couldn't see his head because I was a step down from the kitchen floor. This all happened in an instant.

December 10, 2011

It was about 4:30 a.m. when I awoke. At the end of the bed were three animals – a black cat, a white bird, and a white tiger. I believe the black cat was Sabrina. I think that it was Sabrina because I couldn't see her face, just a side view of her. She was very dim. The white bird was facing the opposite way than Sabrina. It was just sitting upright. The white tiger was looking at me. The tiger had dark gray stripes. None of the three animals moved. The vision lasted several seconds.

December 11, 2011

We were very busy at the store where I was working, and I had made several mistakes. I knew I couldn't make any more without getting into trouble. I thought to myself, "Monica, please help me; my drawer is never going to balance." (Monica is my angel that Barbara Evans told me about.) At that moment a white feather landed right beside my hand. This is one of my signs from Monica. I smiled and put it into my pocket so that I could show Jim when I got home. My drawer did balance at the end of my shift. Thank you, Monica. (I must've lost the feather when I pulled out my tissue because it wasn't in my pocket when I got home. Or, maybe Jim wasn't supposed to see it!)

My visions became so few and far between from this point on that I quit documenting them. I no longer have them at all, and I miss them so much!

Just as I put this idea to paper, zap! I have another vision.

January 4, 2012

I was sitting in church listening to Pastor Beck tell a story during his sermon. All at once, I knew what

I should be learning while I'm on this Earth or my purpose in life as some people call it. I am to improve my attitude towards mentally challenged people.

Pastor Beck's sermon had nothing to do with the mentally handicapped or what our purpose in life is supposed to be.

My daughter-in-law Vicki has a mentally challenged sister who I find very irritating. She talks all the time, saying everything two or three times, and is very loud. She always wants to hug me and I have to make myself do that. On Christmas I just didn't hug her. You can easily see that I have my work cut out for me. I'm sure that this was a big Divine Moment.

Since I'm so sure that this is my aim in life, I have tried to work on this.

There is a bus that brings a group of mentally handicapped people into the store where I work about once a month. Before I received this message they really made me uncomfortable and I was always very glad when they left. Now I talk to them normally, help them with their money, and give them an extra sack when they ask. Sacks seem to be very precious to them.

I thank God for the message He gave me, and the help He's giving me to overcome this uneasiness. I have also been waving at Vicki's sister when I see her at ballgames. The last time I saw her we were at one of the grandchildren's birthday parties. I went right up to her and gave her a big hug. I do think I'm making progress.

January 10, 2012

I woke up earlier than I like to get up so I started to turn over and go back to sleep. I tried to move my legs but I felt a weight on them. It took me only a second to realize it was Sabrina in bed with me. I lay very still, and I could feel her purring and her paws feeling for my legs. I looked down several times to see if I could see her. It was very light in the room but I couldn't see her. I always loved it when she slept with us. She didn't do this very often. I think I moved too much for her to stay in bed with us. I miss her.

February 6, 2012

The way this vision came about was entirely new for me.

I was in the middle of a dream about a boy with whom I had gone through school. I awoke suddenly and I knew there was a vision for me to see. I looked carefully all over the wall I was facing and saw nothing but my pictures. I turned over and there was my vision. It was a two-or three-year-old little girl. She was chubby and dressed as they dressed children in the 1920s and '30s. She also had a "block" haircut that was popular back then. It looked as if she were trying out an automatic-opening door for the first time. She appeared to be about three feet above the floor.

Part 3

Accounts of
Spiritual Phenomenon

by Family and Friends

Rev. Rusty, my son.

"Six to seven months before I accepted the call to preach," Rusty writes, "I felt there was something wrong at church. I didn't know if it was something with the church, or me, so I began praying and asking God to let me know what was wrong or what he wanted me to do. No one knew how or what I was praying about, not even my wife. Time passed and I partially forgot about the prayer.

"Every year the 'Bikers for Christ' have a big motorcycle rally and worship weekend in Zanesville, OH. As my wife and I headed up to the rally, I started having bike trouble. Everything was going wrong. I was ready to turn around and go home. My wife said that I always had fun at the rally and that we should just go on. We finally made it without any more trouble with the motorcycle.

"On Saturday night after church, everyone gathered at the Denny's restaurant to eat. When we were finished eating, my wife and I went back to the motel when the founder of 'Bikers for Christ' came up to me, shook my hand and asked me if I were going to preach in the morning. (He lives in California, and I had never met him before.) I told him that I hadn't planned on it but if God told me to do so, I would.

"As we walked back to the motel, I asked my wife why she thought he had asked me that because I knew that he was fully aware that Barry Mason was preaching in the morning.

"When the weekend was over and we were on our way back home, it came to me what God wanted me to do. He was calling me to preach and what better person to tell me than someone who lived 3000 miles away.

"From that moment on I told God that I was tired of arguing and what ever He wanted done would be done. I have been preaching His Word ever since."

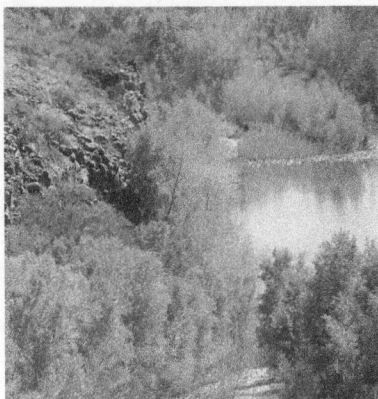

Pop, my grandfather, Entrepreneur *(as told to me by Tootsie Hemry, my mother)*

Pop was in the hospital in a coma. His heart was failing and he was bleeding internally, so we knew it wouldn't be long before he passed to the Other Side. My mother was staying with him as much as possible.

Suddenly, on the sixth evening, Pop opened his eyes, looked way over his head, smiled, and died. Mother suggested that it was probably a relative or even his wife had come to welcome him to the Other Side. It made Mother so happy that she had observed this Godly happening.

Dad, CPA/Entrepreneur

Dad and a friend were touring Europe and visiting my brother in Germany (see also July 1953 above) where he was stationed during the Korean conflict. One day Dad said that he felt something was wrong at home. He called my mother and she told him that I was very ill and in the hospital. Divine Moments find you wherever you are.

Tootsie Hemry, my mother, Housewife

Mother was in the hospital after having a hyster-
ectomy and developed a bad infection. She was
in and out of a coma for several days. When she
finally pulled through this ordeal and was home, she
talked to me about it. She said, "My aunt Carrie
was standing at the door to my room with her arms
held out to me. I was very glad to see her, but I
didn't want to go with her." The interesting thing
about this is, her aunt Carrie died before she was
born. Since there weren't many pictures back then,
I doubt that she ever saw a picture of Carrie either.

Many years later, Mother was dying from breast
cancer. The cancer had metastasized to her spine
and was going to her brain. The doctor said that
she didn't have long to live. I was spending as
much time in Springfield with her as I could. I lived
in Wheelersburg, Ohio, at this time (it's about a
three-hour drive). One day I headed home to check
on the kids and stayed overnight. I went back to
Springfield the next morning.

When I walked into Mother's room, she was smiling. She said, "A very strange thing happened while
you were gone. The Angel of Death was here. He
was over by the door to the bathroom. He wasn't
standing he was just there. Anyway, he said, 'Not
now, but soon.' and then he left." She also told me
that he didn't look like what she thought he would.
He was in a white robe, and she thought he would
be dressed all in black with a black hood.

Doug, my brother, Teacher

I remember hearing Doug talk about Bopy Ivan
when I was young. Doug was seven years old at
that time. As I was writing this book, I began to
think about it. I had read so many stories about
spirit friends appearing to young children.

I called Doug on the phone. He told me that he was
two years old when he "made him up" and it was
kind of a joke. Then he said that he took Bopy Ivan
everywhere with him. He talked to him and they
played together for years. Doug was a little embar-
rassed talking about it, so he made light of it.

If you have read Sylvia Browne's book Psychic
Children, you would have read that she thinks
during a reincarnation, the newly born child retains
the memory of "The Other Side" for up to about
seven years. This is what I think was happening to
Doug. I can't imagine a two-year-old making up a
name like Bopy Ivan.

Sherry, my sister,
Nursing home Dietary Manager

Sherry says, "My first psychic experience was shortly after my father died. I was staying at his house and was sleeping in my mother's old room. While I was sleeping, the phone rang sharply and I answered it. It was my father. He said that he was worried about me and that he didn't know where he was, but he knew he could never come back. I awoke screaming and knew that this was no dream. I felt that he had reached out to me. I can still hear his voice clearly and the emotion in it." (Sherry has been seriously ill since birth and has had many close brushes with death.)

Several years later, Sherry and I went for a medium reading in Dayton, Ohio. This was a group reading and there were about six people in attendance. When the session was almost over, he looked at Sherry and asked if she had lost a child.

"Yes." (Her little girl had died soon after she was born.)

"She is asking where the lighted Christmas decoration is. She says that she likes it."

Sherry replied, "I didn't put it out this year."

Margie, Housewife

"I was seven when my dad died in Cleveland, Ohio," Margie says. "He was forty years old. Mom brought me to West Virginia to live with my grand-mother while she sold our house and worked.

"My bed was a large baby crib (I was small) next to a window. One night, a warm breeze awakened me. I looked out the window and there stood my dad as if he were getting ready to go someplace. He had on his sleeveless undershirt and the dark blue trousers that I last remember seeing him wearing. I jumped out of my bed and ran through the hall and out the back door and stepped down on the large rock that was a makeshift step. It was cool on my bare feet. I ran almost up to Dad and started crying. I begged him to stay, and he smiled and said, "I can't stay, Punkin." (His nickname for me.) "I have a meeting with angels." With that he was gone and I went back to bed.

"The interpretation of that dream came to me sev-eral years later. Dad didn't go to church, although he made sure I did. I wondered about that and was concerned that Dad would not go to heaven. God answered my question about Dad's spiritual status by appearing in the familiar form of my dad so that it would not frighten a seven-year-old child.

"And now I know that God even speaks to children and calms all their little worries."

Loren, Railroad Enthusiast

"This story begins with my wife Shirley's father," writes Loren, "during his last days. He had been ill for a short time in and out of the hospital and finally at the hospice house in Ashland, Kentucky. It was there that I stayed with him at night. Things started to run through my mind. His time is running short. How much longer is he going to be with us?

"Well, we had a bad windstorm that blew leaves and limbs all over his yard just three nights before he passed away. That morning I went down there with my mower and started to clean it up. It was during that time as I was riding the mower that I started thinking how much longer was Pawpaw going to be with us. Then numbers started going through my mind. Number one and another number one and again another number one and yes the fourth number one. I started thinking why number one. As I was riding, the numbers got associated with cards, and I thought sometimes ones are used as aces in some card games. There's only one hand better, it's a straight flush. Then the lights came on. Here Pawpaw was holding four aces in his hand, and the Lord was holding a straight flush in His hand. He was coming to get His child of God. When is this going to take place? Well, remember the four number ones? They became number elevens.

"I had just finished cleaning up the yard and headed for home. When I got there, Shirley told me Christy was coming home and wanted to go to see Pawpaw that night before he got worse. So that evening

102

Christy and I headed to the hospice house. We were there about three hours when the nurse came in to check all of his vitals. She told us we had better call the family in and that things were not looking good. We all spent the night and next day there.

"At the end of the evening, I started thinking about what had gone through my mind the day I was cleaning up his yard, the number ones and elevens. Well, today is November 11 and he passed away at 10:05 p.m. just before the eleventh hour. Were all of these numbers and circumstances just coincidences or what?

"Here's another number that came up – 168. When we left the hospital to follow the ambulance to the hospice house, they took the back way from Belle-fonte Hospital. We thought they would take the better Route 23 to Route 60 to go out back of Ash-land, a straight and much easier ride, but they chose the back way up and down hills. It was bumpy and had lots of curves. That road was known as 168 and Blackburn Rd. This was the road hospice house was on.

"I didn't think too much about that number 168 at the time, but the next morning Shirley and her sister along with Granny were all getting ready to leave and go to the funeral home to make arrangements. Before we left, Granny's brother stopped by on his way to Buckeye Cemetery to show the gravedigger where the lot was. Granny told him to make sure it was lot number 168. As we were at the funeral home and after everything was picked out, the funeral director asked what time we wanted the service, morning or afternoon. All of us said morning. Then he asked what time 9:00 a.m., 10:00 a.m., or 11:00 a.m. All said 11:00 a.m. at the same time. Here is the number eleven again.

"As we were getting ready the morning of the funeral, I was sitting at the kitchen bar eating breakfast. Something kept telling me to go outside and look. This went on for a few minutes, and then I decided to go and look. As I was outside looking around, I noticed that it had rained during the night. Things were still a little wet – nothing any different. I thought, 'What made me come out here?' Then I looked up and there it was the most beautiful rainbow I had ever seen going from our house and down over the top of Shirley's father's home. I hurried to tell Shirley to come and look, but she was getting ready. As I went back outside to look again, it had all but faded out. Well, it takes two things to make a rainbow – rain and sunshine – and it was doing neither at the time. Was there a message here?

"One last thing that I noticed was when we were going to the gravesite at the cemetery, there was a little beagle dog there at the back of the gravesite.

Pawpaw always loved beagle dogs. He had two of them back at the house. After the service, I talked to the fellows who dug the grave. They said the dog came there when they started digging, and as far as they knew it had stayed there ever since. Next morning, I stopped by to make sure everything was in order and I looked around for the dog. It was no-where to be found and it hasn't been seen anywhere since. Did all these things just happen? Was God working through the Holy Spirit?

"Pawpaw's birthday is October 16 and little Lau-ren's birthday is also October 16. (Lauren is my son's daughter.) When Pawpaw saw and held her for the first time, he said, 'This is our little star and she shines ever so bright.' Needless to say Pawpaw's birthday is still celebrated October 16 through our little star."

Barbara C., Housewife/Hospice Volunteer

A Trip to the Hospital

Barbara writes, "I was a stay-at-home mom with three children, three, five, and seven years of age. We lived in Ashland, Ky. I was doing some house cleaning. I was standing on a stepstool hanging drapes. All of a sudden the stool tipped, and I fell to the floor and landed on my side. I sent my son across the street to get the neighbor. They called the paramedics. They took me to King's Daughters' Hospital. I was worrying all the way to the hospital about my children.

"When I got to the hospital, I asked the doctor what was wrong with me. He said it was either my liver or spleen, but he would take care of me. He said that there was a doctor who had just returned from the military, and he could perform the surgery very fast.

"When they raised me on a backboard to take the X-ray, I went into shock. They don't do surgery when you're in shock.

"The next thing I knew, I was in a bed and I could hear them talking. I heard a nurse say I didn't have a pulse. A doctor came in a few minutes later and said, 'Honey, I'm going to give you a shot to start your heart.'

"But in the meantime, I decided I had to stop think-ing about the kids. I was hurting so bad I decided

I'd just give up and go on over to the Other Side. But a voice said to me, 'You're being selfish. What about your children?'

"So I decided to come back to the earth. After I was given six pints of blood that they brought down from Huntington, West Virginia, they said I had ruptured my spleen. I recuperated and still have my life."

The Loss of My Husband

"I had just retired after working many years for the county. My husband was still working and he wanted to go on vacation. He wanted to go to Washington, D.C. We decided to take the train into D.C. the next morning.

"We were doing a lot of walking, just enjoying the sightseeing. On the third day I noticed he was stopping quite often and holding his side. He said his side hurt.

"Do you think you have a hernia?

"Well, maybe.

"I said, 'You know when you walk it hurts.'

"We went back to the hotel early, and being a wife, I was complaining that we wouldn't get to see much of anything with him hurting as he was. At this point, a voice came to me and said, 'This will be your last vacation together.'

When we got home, he had surgery. He had a trip planned in conjunction with his job at Ashland Oil. We had some friends in Lexington with whom we always got together. We were getting ready to go on our trip, and I didn't get ready. I was still thinking about what the voice had said. I had not told him about the voice. Then I thought, 'Well, this isn't really a vacation. It's a business trip.'

"So I got ready, and we went on the trip to St. Louis. We had a good time. He died one month later.

"It was Thanksgiving and he was doing the cooking. I was in the kitchen doing the prep work with him. He had an appointment with his doctor the next day.

"He said, 'I'm going to die before you.'

"You don't know that!

"He turned to face me and said very sadly, 'You know I am.'

"He died later on Thanksgiving Day."

"We always went to our church conferences in Independence, Missouri. After he died, I wasn't going to go.

My friend from Louisville, KY, called and said, 'You are going to the church conference.'

"No I'm not.

"You can stay with us at my daughter's.'

"So I went with them, and about the second day of the conference, our delegation sat way in the back. The handicapped area was near the front of the auditorium. After the service, I had the feeling that I must go down to the handicapped area. The lady from Louisville was handicapped, and she was sitting next to a man that was in a wheelchair too.

"He said, 'I just now heard that your husband died. We didn't know that.'

"His wife had gone through another exit and came around to her husband. As soon as she walked in, she said, 'Oh! I just saw your husband in the back of the auditorium.'

"I don't think so.'

"Her husband said, 'Mary, he died.'

"The tears started flowing, and she said, 'but I did!'

"I asked her what he looked like and she said, 'The same. He had a big name tag on just like the rest of us are wearing. But, he knew something was wrong with me because he said, 'Mary, how are you doing?' She had been having some heart problems. But it was definitely he. What a thrill this was for me!"

Rev. Donald H. Mosher, retired clergy member of St. John Lutheran Church, Powellsville, Ohio

"As a young person," Rev. Mosher writes, "I grew up in a family that was active in our local Lutheran church in Huntington, West Virginia. My father was the unofficial weekly greeter and usher. As kids, my siblings and I attended Sunday School each week and we usually sat near the back of the church so that my dad could join us once the service began and so that he would be ready to serve as an usher when it came time for the offering. I was actively involved in Sunday School, confirmation class, and Luther League youth group, Camp Luther, each summer and became a counselor there.

"Upon graduation from Huntington East High School in 1952, I entered Teachers' College at Marshall University planning to become a high school social studies teacher. I became president of the Lutheran Student Association and worked with other denominational representatives as we developed and built the Campus Christian Center. Near the end of my second year I was drafted into the U.S. Army and sent to Fort Knox, Kentucky for basic training in December 1954.

"Although as a college student I was eligible for a draft deferment, I did not pursue that option because I was struggling with my life's calling, and I felt that two years in the military would help me make an important decision about my ultimate career choice. During my processing, I scored relatively high on the IQ test, and since I had completed two years of college, my sergeant at Fort Knox wanted me to sign up for 'Officers' Candidate School' and consider a career as a commissioned officer.

"At the end of my basic training, the sergeant called me into his office and asked me to tell him which of the three options I wanted to pursue in my military career: 1) Officers' Candidate School for a qualified draftee like myself; 2) advanced infantry training to learn how to use the BAR [ed. Note: Browning Automatic Rifle] and kill those 'chinks'; or 3) advanced training as a clerk and learn how to use the new electric IBM typewriter. Without much forethought or prayer, I said 'Sergeant, give me that IBM!' I was sent to clerk-typist school and upon graduation assigned as a supply clerk in a Battalion Headquarters unit at Fort Bliss, Texas.

"Shortly after arriving on base, I discovered there was a Lutheran chaplain assigned to the chapel near my barracks. I became an active participant in chapel activities and the chaplain asked me if I would assist him by reading the Scripture lessons, serving as acolyte, and assisting him with the distribution of Holy Communion. Having been active in my home congregation and having served in leadership positions in Luther League, church camp, and the Lutheran Student Association, I was honored to be invited to assist him.

"I told him I was considering the ministry as a possible career choice and that was one of the primary reasons why I had not sought deferment from the draft. He encouraged me to read several books by

Lloyd C. Douglas in my spare time. One was *The Robe*, which had been made into a movie that I had seen. The other one was called Dr. Hudson's *Secret Journal*, a book about a man who had a driving accident and unintentionally killed a promising young physician. In remorse for his action and to make amends for this doctor's death, the man felt called to become a physician himself to help others.

"The chaplain reminded me that Douglas was pastor of First Lutheran Church in Lancaster, Ohio, and he had some intriguing religious ideas about how Jesus had taught that when one does things in secret to help others that God will bless his actions openly. Douglas also offered some keen insights into what happened to the adults when a young boy willingly shared his five loaves and two fishes. When Jesus blessed them, he had the crowd sit down and his disciples said over 5000 people were there, and there were twelve baskets of bread and fish left over. The boy had secretly shared his food that he had hidden inside his clothing, but seeing the hungry people, he willingly shared it so that Jesus could feed every one.

"Shortly afterward, the chaplain was reassigned to Korea, and I started attending the local Lutheran church near the base. There was a German immigrant pastor at the church who was a powerful preacher. He had a young assistant pastor who worked with the youth of the military families. His assistant arranged a number of activities that involved those of us on the base who were far from our homes. He had Bible studies, picnics, movie outings, etc., to help us cultivate and develop meaningful relationships. As I participated in such acts, I began to feel God's call to the ministry. It was not some sudden revelation from on high but a natural progression of involvement in the church with a committed home pastor, a military chaplain and other new pastors, church leaders and welcoming members that opened this vista to me.

"Frequently as an active young person in my congregation and as a church camp counselor working with pastors each summer, I had been encouraged by many of them to consider the ministry. However, I was not certain that I had the skill, knowledge, or competence for such a calling. Since I was pondering my future career, I now had time to read, study, and talk with interested chaplains and new pastors about such a calling. I came to believe that God was truly calling me and opening this door for me to enter – if I had the vision and commitment to take that step with His help.

"Since the war was over, if I planned to return to college, I was eligible for an early release from the U.S. Army. I applied for and received the release. Upon returning to Marshall University, I changed my major from social studies in the teachers' college to history and philosophy in the arts and sciences college.

"One day as I walked across campus, Dr. Stewart H. Smith, Marshall's president, was escorting the Rev. Dr. Franklin Clark Fry, president of the United Lutheran Church in America, around campus because he was a guest speaker that week. Dr. Smith, a Lutheran and a member of my home church, introduced me to Dr. Fry as one of our best students and an aspiring pastoral candidate. While I saw no aura around him, Dr. Fry graciously shook my hand and said, 'Welcome to the ministry. The church always needs fine young men like you!'

"I simply share this experience to illustrate that one can experience the power of God's call without necessarily seeing a vision or hearing a voice from on high, such as happened when God called Moses or Samuel or Isaiah or Saul or Martin Luther or any of the other blessed saints whom God has called to serve Him. We each experience our calling in a unique way, and as St. Paul reminds us, God equips us with different gifts to serve Him. It is our task to hear His call and to obey his divine commission faithfully. As John explains in his Gospel, 'To all who received Jesus, who believed in His name, He gave power to become children of God. Even the sinner can become a new redeemed child of God, and be blessed with the Holy Spirit so that we can show love to God and His neighbor.' Following the Beatitudes, Jesus told His followers, 'You are the light of the world... Let your light shine before others so that they may see your good works and give glory to your Father in heaven.' I've tried to shine that light faithfully."

I think this is a wonderful story because it shows that it doesn't take a lightning bolt to know that God is working in our lives. All we need to do is listen.

114

Monica Harlock, Respiratory therapist/ Music teacher

Monica says, "My near-death experience was during the birth of my twins. The pregnancy was fine up until the last month and toxemia set in. That means high blood pressure, leg and ankle swelling, and general discomfort. I worked at the hospital as a respiratory therapist and did lots of walking to take care of my patients. The last two weeks I could not even fit into a pair of shoes. The only shoes I could wear were Dr. Scholl's slip-on clogs. My doctor finally told me that I should now be on bed rest with my legs up. So I went home.

"The day came to deliver the babies after finding out I had been in labor the past two days. The labor came fast and hard. The water broke from only one of the twins, and I was pushing but could not make progress due to the larger twin, a boy, still above his sister who was just not moving out. I became stressed physically from pushing for forty-five minutes. They gave me an epidural that paralyzed me from the waist down. The nurse said the doctor had to get the baby out manually and quickly. While trying to deliver the first twin, a girl, my blood pressure began to drop, and I remember only a few of the details. I remember them starting another IV, constant blood pressure monitoring, and getting the crash cart, which was used when the patient needed emergency medical attention.

"The next event was an experience I will never for-get. I was watching everything that was going on from above the people in the room. I was floating weightless, calm, no pain, no fear or worries not even about the babies – a peace that was unexplainable. My mind was free of this world. I could see myself laying there, the nurses on each side of me, and another assisting the doctor. The incubators were lighted, and they were equipped with blankets and breathing bags.

"I had prayed throughout my pregnancy for the Lord to help me have healthy babies. I felt Him give me that peace that all was going to be all right. There were images surrounding the nurses, and now I believe they were spiritual angels helping them with their care of the twins and me.

"The next time I was conscious, they were showing me the babies and telling me I had a beautiful boy and girl. I had to lie flat, and they had to work with the babies. Later I found out that Matthew had to be resuscitated and have oxygen to help his breathing. Melissa was fine at first but later gave them a scare, turning blue, so that she too had to have oxygen intermittently to help with her breathing.

"The precious Lord saved me from knowing all of that at the time. He held me gently in His arms and gave me peace. I am thankful that I came back to my body and have had the pleasure of bringing up my twins and our other three children and now grandchildren. I truly know that when one is facing death, there is nothing to be afraid of and that I have heavenly angels around me all the time helping me through all life's events."

Probably a Ghost Spirit.

"After the kids had gone to bed, my husband, Richard, shared with me one evening about his experiences with the spiritual realm. We had been watching television, and something came on to prompt
him to tell me. Both experiences were while he was
living in England. One experience happened as a
teenager and the other when he was a young man.
It was evening when the first experience happened.
He thought he heard something and went to the
window to look out. It was a very cold night, and
there was frost on the inside of the window. They
did not have central heat and upstairs was usually a
bit colder.

He said he felt a chill in the room and from behind
him he felt a movement. He saw a figure, and as
it passed him the temperature dropped even more.
Richard was covered in goose bumps from head to
toe. As quickly as the figure passed he felt a sick-
ening feeling deep in his gut. He said although the
spirit did not hurt him, he knew it was not a good or
Godly spirit."

Richard's grandfather's visit

"The second experience was a touch on his shoulder. He was again in his bedroom, the same room
as before. He was standing near the window. The
gentle pressure he felt on his shoulder from behind
was a warm feeling. A good and peaceful calm
came over him and he had the awareness that it was
his grandfather letting him know that he was fine.

117

He did not see anything; just felt the presence and the touch of the heavenly spirit."

Richard's spirit sighting

"After we were married and we had moved into our home in Arizona, Richard was standing in the kitch-en, and he said when he glanced down the hallway, he saw a man walk across the hall and into our laun-dry room. He was fully dressed and did not look at him. There was no change in temperature like the other time he had experienced it. It was just a spirit walking through our home as if the walls were not there. Richard had no fear or feeling of good or bad. He said he did not think too much about it. He did ask me if I had seen anything unusual in the house. I said, 'No, why?' Then he told me about it. I immediately prayed that I would NEVER see anything like that, and I haven't. Richard said it did not bother him. He knew we had spirits all around us. That is written in the Bible, God's holy word."

Richard's appearance to our son, Greg

"My husband, Richard, died on a Saturday in Janu-ary of 2011 from a long struggle with bone marrow cancer. He was a young fifty-six and very healthy. We had spoken about him coming back to allow one or more of his family to know that he was all right in Heaven. We both have very strong beliefs in Jesus Christ as our Savior and God, our Father, and the Holy Spirit.

"Our prayer was answered. After his death he first

118

appeared to our son Greg in Arizona. Richard was
sitting on Greg's living room couch one Sunday.
Greg said he woke up and walked out of his bedroom and there was Dad sitting in his Dr Pepper
pajama pants and his white tank top. He looked
great! Good color, he had been so very pale and he
told Greg he was okay and nodded his head. Then
he was gone."

Granddaughter Aubralyn's experience

"The next appearance was to our granddaughter
who was two years old at the time. Her mommy
was holding her and noticed that she was staring at
something. When she asked her, she told her mommy she was looking at Papa. She asked Aubralyn
what Papa was doing. She said he was watching
the fish. They have a huge aquarium in their dining
room. Aubralyn had several encounters with Papa
Richard where he played peek-a-boo with her, and
she laughed out loud. She sees him often, and when
asked what he looks like, she simply says he looks
like Papa. She has a close bond with him and is
always happy to see him."

Richard's Goodbye

"The next time he appeared was four months later in
England. His mother, sister, brother-in-law, and
nephew were all gathered around Richard's father's
grave. They were there to spread Richard's ashes
on his father's grave. When they were finished and
were walking away, Lee, his nephew, turned and
looked back at the grave and saw Richard standing

beside the grave. He was dressed in a white robe and looked very young, maybe in his thirties. He smiled and nodded to Lee and then vanished in a blink of an eye."

Doug Riley, Owner of Riley's Equipment Sales and Photographer

"Meetings are not my favorite way to spend a weekend!" Doug says. "Since this meeting was to take place close to Lake Erie, I took my camera hoping the meeting would be over early and I could take a few pictures.

"The meeting was over early and the weather was great for late September. I was driving my Jeep, and I was hoping I could find a place where I could access the beach. It didn't take long for me to realize that there was no public access to the beach along that area. I was getting worried that I wouldn't be able to get to the beach but I kept driving in the same direction. I finally reached a small town called Avon Lake. I found a small park with a foot access to the lake. I parked the Jeep and grabbed my camera. I had my Canon 7D with a 28–300 Pro lens. This is a rather large set up (more on this later).

"I made my way to the beach. The shoreline was not very extensive at this point. I could see maybe a few hundred yards at most. I saw an old tree that had washed up on the beach. I made the best of this small opportunity and snapped several pictures of the tree. I saw several gulls and took several more pictures. I was thinking this was probably going to be the extent of this weekend's photo op. Rather downhearted, I made my way back to the park.

"The sun was setting low in the western sky. I decided I'd just look around the park until I saw that

magic moment in light that makes great pictures.
I noticed an older gentleman walking a small dog.
He was looking my way and motioning for someone
to come to him. I didn't think he meant me since I
didn't know anyone in this area. I just continued on
my way. I was close to the bench that was facing the
lake. I heard a voice from behind me say, 'Would
you come sit with me and talk for a few minutes?'
It was the gentleman with the little dog. I said,
'Yes' and asked him if he had been motioning to me
a while before. He said yes he was.

"I apologized for having walked on, and I said that I
thought he had been motioning to someone else. He
said that was okay and we sat down on the bench.
He said he noticed by my camera that I was more
than just a point and shoot photographer. He began
telling me that he had been a professional photographer over forty years and had been retired for some
time. Now he just carried a small point-and-shoot
camera, which he pulled from his coat pocket and
casually showed to me. He pointed over his shoulder and said he lived with his son across the road
from the park since his wife had passed away a few
months before. He said he liked to walk his dog
and watch the sunset.

"As we sat talking, the sun was brushing across his
face making a very nice photo. As I was about to
ask if I could take his picture, he asked if I minded
if he took my picture? I told him no one ever asked
to take my picture and it would be fine with me. He
asked me to look up, and then look to the side with
my eyes to the right, then eyes to the West as he

snapped away. Then it was my turn to take his picture. He struck a pose; I did not have to say a word – just click away. We sat and talked until the sun had sunk into the lake.

"As we parted, we exchanged our addresses and e-mail addresses and promised to send each other the pictures we had taken. I sent my pictures and a short e-mail in a couple of days. Five weeks passed with no reply from him. I thought something might have happened and thought I would try to contact him.

"Then a large envelope arrived by US mail. In the envelope was a black matted picture. As I opened it up, there was this beautiful picture of a lake in Michigan. It was the one that the man in the park, Demerti Lazaroff, had told me was his favorite picture that he had ever taken. It was early morning as the sun was coming up. He told me that as he arrived at the lake, he had startled a flock of ducks. He took the picture of the ducks as they flew up from the lake. The water was dripping from their feet, and the wings were beating. The sun was just perfect, and I could see why he said this was his favorite picture.

"All photographers have a favorite picture that they have taken. What really touched me so much was that Demerti was probably up in his eighties, and this picture was probably taken in the mid fifties. I was judging this by the type of matting he had used. He never told me the exact date he took the picture, but the fact that he would send his original print of his favorite picture to a complete stranger was very touching for me.

"In the envelope there was also a biography that was written by his wife. It told of Demerti's accomplishments during his life and the things that had taken place in his photography including the awards he had been given. What I thought was so fantastic about our encounter was that I was in a hurry to get away from my business meeting, and it seemed that I couldn't find a way into the lake. Then I found this small city park just by chance. I walked into the park and down to the beach, took the pictures, and came back up. When I came back up, I was thinking that this was going to be a very uneventful picture-taking session. Nothing was going to be special. I had looked forward to taking a lot of pictures around the lake, and now I was disappointed. Then there was Demerti!

"Why he picked me to sit down with me and share some great stories about his life was something I'll always wonder about. What really impressed me about him was that he was talking just like anyone else whom you would meet. Most people who have accomplished a small part of what Demerti had would be bragging. Demerti was just stating his accomplishments as if anyone could have done them. It was just as if he were opening up his life and letting me come in. I felt very special for that. It didn't dramatically change my life, but it was a special meeting. The two of us just sat and talked, and the things that we shared were so personal. He got up and walked away with his gorgeous little

124

ball of fur dog. He had this little shuffle to him.

"I still can't get over how lucky I was, all of the things that happened to let me have this meeting with him: the business meeting taking longer than I had hoped, not finding a way onto the beach for miles then finding this little park. I think it was meant for me not to find the place to go to the beach and be able to take the other pictures that I had in my mind. It was meant for me to meet Demerti. I believe some people call these Divine Moments. As I thought back over this encounter and all of the special things Demerti told me, it was as if he wanted to share the events of his life with someone who would appreciate them before he passed over, and possibly that person would tell his story to others."

Rev. Evan D. Fisher

"Somewhere in the mid-1950s," Rev. Fisher writes, "I picked up a magazine in a dentist's waiting room. The article that grabbed my attention claimed that folks with both a law degree and an accounting degree could make big money. The formula was straightforward: approach presidents of middle-sized companies and offer to review their tax returns and split the savings. I liked it. As I thought about it, I saw other benefits: I figured clients arrested for cheating on their taxes would likely be taken into custody between 8a.m. and 5p.m. so it should not be necessary to get out of bed in the middle of the night to bail them out of jail. Second, if a client were convicted of breaking tax laws, he or she would not be executed so I would escape having that on my conscience.

"My plan for a career seemed clear until the notion of ministry came to me. I was pretty sure pastors did not make as much money as tax attorneys (I still believe that). So I determined that I might be a tax lawyer and a Sunday school teacher. By my junior year in college, I knew I had a problem.

"The more I thought about tax law, the more unsettled was my life. The more I thought about ministry, the more life made sense. If that constitutes a call I had one – not an audition let alone a vision. It seems to me a strong sense of vocation. After serving two congregations for a total of forty years, I am enjoying guest preaching in retirement. If I had a choice, it was the right one for me."

126

Robin Stanley, Program Director at a substance treatment center

Robin says, "When you asked me to share with you a personal mystical experience, I struggled to narrow it down to something I thought might be interesting to you or to others. My life is truly a series of almost daily magical experiences as I continually seek guidance from my spirit guides and elders to help me through this life. I often see, feel, and experience their presence in the smallest details of my life. However, I feel my holiest task is to share with others the gifts I have been given. I hope that the following story can give hope or inspiration to a weary soul who is struggling with tragedy or the unforeseen in life.

"During winter and spring of 2002, my family was going through a difficult time as my husband Greg was between jobs with no prospects on the horizon, we were in the middle of building a house, and I was finishing a grueling course to complete a bachelor's degree while working full time to sustain our blended family.

"In an effort to reward myself for finishing the degree, in late April I planned to pay a weekend visit to my friend Kathleen in Toledo, Ohio. We were having a marvelous time just talking and catching up when she suggested we visit a new age shop called Rainbow and Roses that she frequented. On that day, a lady was in the shop reading tea leaves. I had never had my tea leaves read and was excited about hearing what they had to say. Having just completed a long sought after milestone in my life and hoping that our worst days would soon be behind us, I really wanted to hear the leaves say that I was entering a prosperous new phase in my life, etc. I could not have been more off base. When the lady told me that the leaves said that I would be going through a difficult time and that I would be working harder than I ever had in my life, I thought for sure that the leaves were mistaken. Surely they were referring to the phase I was in now and had just come through because, quite frankly, I had never worked so hard in my life as I had to that point, both finishing college and building a house while keeping our family together and financially afloat.

"Kathleen and I both had our leaves read, shared with each other the divining, laughed, went to dinner, and I soon forgot about the reading. I left for home on Sunday morning and reached home about 2:00 p.m. No one was home so I took the opportunity to take a short nap on the couch. After closing my eyes for only a few minutes, I was gently awakened by an angel who appeared illuminated and suspended in the air over me. She spoke no words but just looked at me as I, scared but enchanted, was waiting for her to speak. But she did not speak – not that day anyway. After a few moments, she dissolved in a beam of light. I was thrilled by the visit and felt honored by the presence, but I could not connect the presence to anything specific – not yet, anyway.

"A couple weeks later, my suspicions about receiving the wrong message from the tea leaves were confirmed when Greg finally got a job with a company in Columbus, Ohio. My nagging fears about the reading were put to rest for all I could see was smooth sailing ahead.

"But that was not to last. Greg planned on staying in Columbus during the week and coming home on weekends. On Friday morning of the first week as I was looking forward to his return from the work week, I received a call from a hospital in Columbus informing me that Greg had collapsed while at work. He had suffered a brain aneurysm with a massive bleed.

"For the next several months as Greg moved between life and death, I came to realize that the message from the tea leaves and my visit from the angel were to be my comfort for this period of my life. The angel's presence has given me reassurance in the months and years since just knowing that I was not alone during that horrific time. And the tea leaves were not mistaken. As others who have experienced tragedy can affirm, over the next months and years, our family developed a new level of strength and resilience in response to our family's tragedy. During times of discouragement, I held and still hold fast to the assurance that I had support in and from another realm.

"Greg returned home in late November of that year in a wheel chair, incontinent, and unable to feed, bathe, or care for himself in any real way. After hard work, he was able to use a walker and finally a cane. The folowing months and years of struggle for my husband and me were the most difficult and triumphant times of my life. However, he never recovered his mental capacity and so his physical recovery was limited. After a long, difficult battle, Greg left this life in July 2010. His beautiful spirit and influence live on.

"I could never have survived the ordeal without the knowledge and assurance that we were not alone in our struggle but had the support of not only those in this realm but in alternate realms alongside us."

Dr. John Simon, Professor at Shawnee State University, Portsmouth, Ohio/ farmer.

Cows

"I have a small farm," Dr. Simon writes, "on which I raise cattle and sorghum cane. One day I heard a commotion near the barn where I store the sorghum cane until it's time to make the molasses. Cows love this cane. This day, the cows had broken down the gate and were happily munching on my cane. I went running and screaming and swearing trying to get those cows out of my sorghum. Of course, the cattle scattered everywhere. I stopped carrying on and prayed to the farmer's patron saint, St. Isidore. Almost at once my neighbor happened by and helped me get the cows out of the sorghum and back in the fence." (This is a Divine Moment in action.)

Cats

"I have a lot of little critters that don't necessarily belong to me, but I feed them and they stay around and keep me company. Among these critters are a number of cats. Cats are very curious animals, and can be very mischievous. They also love to sleep and play in, on, and around my pickup truck. This day the wing window was open just a crack, enough though that one of the cats must've gained entry. I needed to go somewhere in my truck that day, so I went out to the truck and expected my keys to be in the ignition where I always leave them. They weren't there. I looked all over the truck floor, seats, back floor, etc. No keys, I thought, those darn cats.

131

The best thing I knew to do was to pray to St. Anthony. As I walked back to my house, there, some forty feet away from the truck, tucked in next to the porch foundation lay my keys. Thank you, St. Anthony."

Allison Neff Kalb, City Parks Manager.

1940's

"I want to tell you about some dreams I have had," Allison says, "that have made me believe there is truly life after death and that life goes on. I've always been my dad's barber since I was probably fourteen or fifteen years old. About every two to three months he would want me to cut his hair really short. My brother would be sitting there whispering, 'Alley, just take a little off. Don't make it so short.'

"As Dad got older, I would worry and think that this might be his last hair cut. He had congestive heart failure, and by the time he reached seventy-seven, it became more and more apparent that he didn't have a lot of time. So every time I cut his hair, he would say, 'Now make me look good because this may be my last time, and I want to look good.'

"A few years before my dad passed away, I had a dream. I knew without a shadow of a doubt that it was real and I had gone to a different place.

"In the dream, my uncle Leonard, who was very close to my dad, told me that he was very tired and wanted to know if I would walk home with him. I was a bit confused about him wanting me to walk him home since he had many family members that were close to him. But I told him I would. The first thing I knew, we were climbing this beautiful green grassy hill. As we topped this hill, we came to an opening like a doorway – beautiful, gorgeous blue sky, a bluer blue than I had ever seen.

"As soon as we went in through the door, Uncle Leonard's whole attitude changed. His physical body changed, and he looked so young and so happy and not tired any more. As he walked in, there were a lot of people sitting in a circle, and he started greeting everyone.

"As I looked in through the door, I looked to the left and there was a funny-looking white bed. It was very strange looking. It didn't look comfortable at all. It curled up on the sides. My dad was lying in that bed with a sheet pulled up to his neck. I didn't want to look at him because I knew that he was gone. I didn't feel really sad, and I didn't go over and stand over him. I was more concerned about going over to greet everybody.

"I looked around the circle and saw my grand-mother sitting about 5 o'clock. I was so glad to see her since she had been gone quite a while. I went over and sat down beside her and hugged her. She looked so happy and so good. Then I looked around at all the people and they were all my aunts and uncles who had passed.

"There was one man who was sitting about 12 o'clock, and I didn't recognize him. He looked very young and I just didn't recognize him. I asked my grandma and she told me that it was my grandpa. He looked at me with a big smile. I asked grandma, 'Does he know me?' She told me that he had

134

always known me. Then she said she had some-thing to tell me. She got really serious and she always talked with a twang and very slowly. She said, 'I want you to quit waistin all them purty days.' That's how she talked.

"I assured her that I wouldn't waste any more of the pretty days. Then she turned around, and I noticed that her dress was split up the back. I said, 'Oh, grandma, your dress is ripped. Sit back down so no one will see.'   She just smiled and said, 'They do that.'

"I looked and I couldn't see a body in the dress. I thought that was really strange. She told me that it was time for me to go back now, but thanks for bringing Leonard home.

"This was a very intense dream, but I knew what it meant; Dad is going to die and Uncle Leonard was going to die. It's going to be okay though because they will be with everyone they know and love. It'll be a happy time for them, but I didn't want them to die. I figured that Uncle Leonard would die first because Dad was still alive on that bed.

"I told my mom about the dream but no one else. Mom told me that funeral directors often split the clothes at the funeral home because it makes it eas-ier to dress the deceased. I expected the deaths to happen soon, so every time Dad or Uncle Leonard would get sick, I'd think, 'This is it.' But several years went by without anyone dying.

"In May of 2003, my dad called me and asked me to come out and give him a hair cut. Several things had happened the previous two weeks before Dad called. Someone had given me two tickets to a B.J. Thomas concert. I had not been a concertgoer, but since I liked B.J. Thomas, I would go. I liked B.J. Thomas because at the time Dad was injured at the steel mill, his favorite song was 'I'm So Lonesome I Could Cry,' by Hank, Sr.

"There were eight of us children, and Dad would come every night and kiss each one of us and then turn out our lights. Because he was in the hospital so long after his accident, I was really missing this. I got the idea to call the radio station that I knew Dad listened to every night and requested that they play 'I'm So Lonesome I Could Cry.' They didn't have the Hank Williams' version, but they did have the B.J. Thomas version.

"My sister and I went to the concert and the tickets were for way up in the back. At the end of the concert, B.J. said that his dad had passed, and he was going to sing his dad's favorite song. He said he missed his dad so much and he'd give anything if he could just talk to him one more time. He started playing 'I'm So Lonesome I Could Cry.' Mary and I looked at each other and started crying. After the concert I wanted to get his autograph. By the time we got down to the main floor, everyone else was already in line. We were the last ones.

"So we waited and finally got to him. We told him we knew he was trying to relay a message to the
136

audience about God's love and spiritualism and that we had gotten the message. Then we told him about Dad's accident and how we had his record played every night through the radio station. He had tears in his eyes. He said, 'That's the sweetest thing I have ever heard. It gives new meaning to my song.'

"He asked if we had ever read the Aquarian Gospel of Jesus Christ. I said no, but that I would get the book and read it. He asked if he could give me a kiss on the cheek. Of course, I said, 'YES!'

"The next day was Mothers' Day. Dad called me and asked me to get Mommy a dozen roses from him. I suggested we get pink. He said, 'That would be perfect!' Dad was not the kind of person who gave flowers. The next day when I delivered the flowers, Dad was sitting on the porch. He got up and I thought how small and fragile he looked. When he gave the flowers to Mom, she got tears in her eyes. The gift touched her more than anything he had ever given her before.

"On May 20th, Dad called me and asked me to come cut his hair. Just before I left my house, my sister called me and said Dad had been taken to the hospital. I immediately went to the hospital. I asked the attending nurse where Dad was and she asked me to wait a minute she had to talk with someone.

"She returned with the chaplain. They took us back to the Family Room and then I heard them call 'code blue.' The minister came back into the room, and I asked him, 'Is that for my dad?' He said, 'Yes, but they got him back again.'

"Now it was finally sinking in that they didn't think Dad was going to make it. Dad died as we were getting on the elevator to go see him.

"They took us to where he was. He as lying there and his hair was all messed up. Since he was so particular about his hair and I had always fixed it, this really bothered me. The funeral director told me that I could cut his hair after he was dressed. After they prepared me for seeing him in the prep room, they took me back, and when I went in, there was Dad lying on the high, hard prep table covered up to his chin with a white sheet. Immediately, I remembered the dream."

Pam DeCamp, Professional Photographer and Writer

The Wisdom of Marbles and Four-leaf Clovers

Pam tells me, "There is a saying that 'angels live among us' and they protect and provide inspiration at times when we need it most. There have been many times during my life that I have been 'blessed' by these angels in times that I've needed them most.

"Growing up in the 1960's and 1970's was very different from the way it is today. There were no Internet, iPods, Nintendos or other portable electronic devices to occupy our time and minds. I was an only child, so entertainment was up to me. When I was at home, I had my mom's old collection of 45's (large vinyl disks for those too young to relate) and an RCA Victor record player. Our basement was unfinished, so I would spend hours roller skating and listening to Rick Nelson, Bobby Darin, Pat Boone, and yes, Elvis!

"Every Sunday we would go to my grandmother's house for dinner and to visit her. I was fortunate enough to own a transistor radio with an ear phone (singular – EAR PHONE – no stereo in those days, just mono) and would listen to the local rock station WIOI. As a teenager I began questioning 'why' should I go for the weekly visit. My mother always said, 'You will appreciate the time you spend there.' This is where the adventure begins!

"My grandmother had a farm – lots of buildings to

explore! There were the barn, garage, chicken
coop, out house, smoke house, and even a cellar. If
I was good, I could even go upstairs to the second
floor of the house and check out all the finds in the
bedrooms.

"My biggest and always most interesting finds were
the marbles that seemed to materialize out of no-
where in the yard around the house. I loved finding
the marbles! They were always so pretty and the
sun made them shine. I even found old clay ones!
Of course, it was 'finders keepers.' Grandma was
always very generous with anything I 'discovered'
and was very willing to part with items. I acquired
dishes, crocks, and even little odds and ends like
vases and framed pictures. My treasures were those
uncovered in the yard – marbles!

"As I became older, I started exploring the yard
for those mystical four-leaf clovers. I still think
that was a ploy just to keep me occupied. I started
finding them! There were great big ones down by
the orchard and even the smaller ones in the yard. I
pressed them between waxed paper and put them in
my Bible. These were treasures as well.

"As a child you do not give much thought to the
sequence of events that occur in your life. Much is
taken for granted. I began to appreciate those visits
to grandma's house. I could tell she was becoming more fragile and frail. She was not a 'hug and
kisser' but I would run and give her a kiss goodbye
as we would leave. I still remember how her house
smelled, the taste of the fried chicken and cobbler,
140

and how everything looked.

"Grandma passed away when I was thirteen. I was sad and really struggled during the time. When we are that age, we tend to deal with grief differently than we do as an adult. There is so much about death we do not understand, but we know it is inevitable.

"After grandma passed away, I was awakened by a strange, surreal dream. Grandma was standing at the foot of my bed. Her standing there was odd because Grandma had always been in a wheelchair and had had a leg amputated several years before her death. This was unsettling and comforting at the same time. She told me 'Everything will be all right' and then she vanished. I felt at peace but was also really unsure of what had just happened.

"One day, while visiting Grandma's grave, I was scouring the ground looking for those elusive four-leaf clovers when I saw a glint of something next to the headstone – a marble!

"Angels do live among us and do provide comfort. I know that my grandma is watching over me, and she leaves little clues behind to show me she loves me and that she is still watching over me – and, yes, I've found four-leaf clovers on her grave."

Charles Clevenger, Professional Photographer, and Published Poet

Undying Love

It seems as if a silent voice
Beckons me into her room.
Momentarily frozen in thought.
I hesitate – memories flood my soul.

It had been her room – her sanctuary.
It was my mother's room;
And how dare I, yes me,
Her grown-up-brat child, intrude?
But the silent voice inaudibly persists:
"Come, there is something you must see."

Hypnotized, I am drawn to a scarred old dresser.
Hesitantly, but subconsciously, I quietly open
The middle drawer.
Neatly folded, dainty, lace-edged –
There it is, what the silent voice wants me to see…
A lesson to absorb.

Tear-stained smudges – hers and mine,
Faint scent traces of powder and rouge,
Nose-wipe smears, unwashed,
Bring memories of shared pain – and joy.
My mother's old handkerchief, lacy and stained,
Bring memories of a love that has never died.
I close the drawer – and wipe a tear.

-Charles Clevenger

Barbara Larter, Librarian/Writer/Poet/Photographer

My friend, Charlie Clevenger, invited me to the Phoenix Writers in Portsmouth, Ohio. I didn't know that they were mainly poets. I had never written a poem, so I felt rather out of place. Charlie kept telling me that I could write poetry. He said, "Anyone can write poetry!"

On the way home I kept hearing these two phrases in my brain: "A baby born too soon," and "To a mother too old." I couldn't understand why I kept thinking of these two phrases.

When I went to bed that evening, I was still thinking of these phrases and finally it came to me, "Those could be the beginning of a poem."

The next afternoon, as I lay down for my nap, the rest of the poem came to me – just like that – all at once. I thought, 'I'd better get up and write this down because I'll never remember it.' I know now that God wrote this poem through my hands. Thank you, God.

IN THE EYES OF THE BEHOLDER

A baby born too soon,
To a mother too old.
She had scales all over her head.
Her big toes were way too long.
Her fingers were long.
Her chest made a "V"
And she couldn't see.
We thought she was perfect.

She had a brain aneurysm.
Heart was weak.
Her growth rate was too fast.
We thought she was perfect.

She walked when she was one.
The doctor said, "Impossible!"
She rode a bike when she was six.
The doctor said, "Impossible!"
She dove off a cliff.
The doctor said, "Impossible!"
We thought she was perfect.

She played with regular kids.
She went to regular school.
She rode the bus to school.
The kids put her on the wrong bus,
And they laughed.
She fell off curbs
And they laughed.
She graduated with her class.
We knew she was perfect.

                    -Barbara Larter   February 13, 2012

I sincerely hope that my book has brought comfort
and hope to those of you who have lost loved ones.
Be assured that all of the stories are written from
the hearts of the people who wrote them. When you
have Divine Moments or Visions, they are so real
that you just can't keep them to yourself.

I pray that you will have many Divine Moments
throughout your lifetime and if you'd like to share
your stories, please write me at:

info@DivineMomentsBook.com

Barbara Larter